KOBLET

+

KUBLER

CYCLING'S FORGOTTEN RIVALRY

GARETH CARTMAN

First published in Great Britain by Gareth Cartman, Distribution by Amazon KDP and IngramSpark.

"HUGO WAS MY DOPING"
FERDY KUBLER

PREAMBLE

Hello. I'm guessing that you fall into one of three categories of reader here – you're the avid cycling nut who has heard of both Ferdy Kübler and Hugo Koblet, and you've probably got a tonne of cycling biographies. Or you have a passing interest in the Tour and you've maybe seen their names without knowing much about them. Perhaps, like me twenty years ago, you confused the two K's. Or I've given you a copy personally because I like you, and you actually have no interest in cycling. But thank you for being polite and taking it into your home.

Whichever group you fall into, what you're about to read is the story of two very different men in a unique period of cycling history, and while my explanations here are mostly for the latter of the three categories of reader, I do hope they're useful for everyone.

We tend to wax lyrical about the 'Golden Era' of cycling, and you can have your opinion on when that started and when it ended, but for most people it's the era during which the legendary Italian rider Fausto Coppi was racing at his peak. This period, roughly from 1947 to 1955, was dominated by five men – Fausto, obviously. Gino Bartali, his great rival, who had won the Tour de France before the war years. Louison Bobet, who won the '53, '54 and '55 Tours, and our two K's, Ferdy and Hugo.

It was an era during which cycling was partly imaginary. There was no television coverage, so the average fan had to make do with a glimpse of their heroes riding past them on the road – or the copious write-ups by journalists who, frankly, saw little more than the fans themselves and instead saw themselves as writers of prose, sometimes poetry. Journalists were here to paint a picture as much as report on the action. It is often through their eyes that we see riders such as Fausto, Ferdy, Louison, Gino and Hugo – and is perhaps why we can never compare this era of cycling history to, say, the Eddie Merckx era of the 60s and 70s.

Cycling – whether it be on road or track (velodromes) – was the sport of the era across mainland Europe. Nothing even comes close, not even football. Fans felt a proximity to their heroes, partly through the legends penned by those prosaic journalists, but mainly because they were men of humble backgrounds who were just like the rest of us. Fausto Coppi and Ferdy Kübler were born a month apart in what for us might seem like appalling poverty, but at the time was common across the whole of Europe. Gino Bartali was a pious individual from a pious country, but you'd commonly find him drinking all night and chain-smoking. Just like the rest of us.

You'll find hundreds of books about Coppi and Bartali, and I'd urge you to read them all, even if some of their content is untrue or embellished. There is little to prove that Gino Bartali was ferrying forged documents hidden inside his bicycle frame, but if you want the legend, you can have the legend. And yet you won't find many about Ferdy and Hugo. Which is strange, considering that Ferdy Kübler won the Tour de France, the World Championships, Bordeaux-Paris, innumerable Tours of Switzerland and Romandie, the Ardennes Classics twice, and considering that Hugo won the Giro d'Italia and the Tour de France before his unfortunate decline. You will find a German-language film about Hugo, and I'd urge you to watch this, it really is quite lovely, but it only gives you part of the story.

I've spoken to many people during the writing of this book, and many people have also avoided me. Waltraut, I'm looking at you. But thanks for pointing me towards your book on Amazon. I do often wonder whether discussions of Hugo are forbidden in Switzerland, although I am indebted to Hanspieter Born for his interpretation of events. As someone who was close to both riders, I have aligned myself to his point of view which, after having brushed up on my German and read all of the biographies available, I believe to be the truth.

What I didn't want to do was produce a dry biography that tells, race-by-race, what happened. I wanted to get under the skins of the riders and, like in We Rode All Day, give them a voice. But more than that, I wanted others of that Golden Era to have a voice and show us more about the characters of the two men, how they were perceived by others, how their actions affected others. The men and women of the era form as much a part of this book as Ferdy and Hugo themselves. I may have invented some dialogue, and I may have attributed some emotions, but factually speaking, there is little in this book that is not true – these races did happen, and they happened in the manner in which I have described.

It's also important to point out that Ferdy and Hugo were more than just bike racers – they represented different sides of Switzerland, both liberal and conservative. Or rather, that they were claimed by those sides and their rivalry was not a simple case of modernity versus traditionalism, their rivalry was complex and veered between outright hate and friendship. It's tempting to paint a picture of two riders forever at odds with each other, but this was not always the case.

I do hope that Switzerland forms more than just a backdrop to this book. We don't usually associate Switzerland with bike racing, although Ferdy and Hugo did their utmost to change this, as has Fabian Cancellara in later years. We often associate Belgians with being hard men, Frenchmen with being sprinters or angry Bretons, Italians and Spaniards with being whippet-thin climbers. But the Swiss? Rather hard to pin them down. That's not to say that they don't have a cycling heritage, we just tend to look elsewhere.

It may also be useful to explain the cadences of the cycling year, especially for those who fall in category three and have found this book in their Christmas stocking. Again, thanks for being so polite and taking it into your home.

The road season typically begins in spring with Classics, or one-day races of around 250km, and there are also some week-long 'stage' races in Italy, before the 'Grand Tours' start. In this era, those Grand Tours were France and Italy, and we could also count Spain's 'Vuelta', even though it took a while for the top riders of the era to take part. Those races would last 3 weeks. Once the Grand Tours were over, riders would focus on one-day races again such as Lombardia, or even the World Championships which takes place in a different country every year. There are some time trialling events such as the Grand Prix des Nations which no longer takes place today, where riders are timed for the same course but race individually – fastest man wins. And there are criteriums – plenty of them – of no importance in the racing calendar, but of great importance to a rider's wallet. They are often staged in towns with many laps and a pre-ordained script.

There is also the track season, which tends to come alive in the winter when the road cyclists are done with theirs and are looking for a pay day.

Velodromes can be open all year round, and host a variety of competitions from sprints to Six Day races where riders are expected to race 24 hours a day for six days (mercifully, in teams of two so they can get some sleep).

As most of the men on bikes at the time were from humble backgrounds, any opportunity to make money would be welcome, so during the winter you would often find the riders of this Golden Era on the track. Aside from the machinery and the equipment available to riders, I think this is one of the biggest differences between today's athletic rider and the riders of the Golden Era – the money. While we might have Lachlan Morton riding unsupported across Europe, he still did it on a £10,000 Cannondale. Ferdy Kübler was so poor that he made his first set of handlebars out of an inner tube and some sand, only to see his father saw the contraption in half anyway. Riders saw cycling as work, work that paid better than the factory. They may have been the last of their kind.

And so to Ferdy and Hugo – the last of their kind, too. This book has taken me over two years to write, and I probably spent the first year writing, ripping it up, writing again, ripping it up and so on and so on. I have received much encouragement, and thanks goes out especially to James Spackman for pointing me in the right direction so many times, to my wife for putting up with me tapping away at the keyboard for far too long, to Feargal McKay who provided me with reading matter on the Six

Day races which therefore provided me with more delightful rabbit holes than I dare care to mention, and to innumerable others who have contributed in no small measure, you know who you are.

PAST
HISTORIC

HUGO: *There was a time, long before the racing, long before it all went wrong, when I would ride with my friends down those wide city-centre streets of Zürich, me with my baker's basket slung over my back. We would dodge tramlines, if you fall you lose, last boy riding wins. We would pick ourselves up, dust ourselves down and sprint to the road markings outside the bakery, then to the jeweller's or the watchmaker's, and I would get my nose as close to the front wheel as I could, my back arched like a camel. I would spit and curse and laugh and joke and make faces like I was being pushed through a meat grinder.*

I was pretending to be you, Ferdy. Can you believe that? Perhaps not. You see, I snuck into the Oerlikon velodrome that day the world gave birth to Ferdy Kübler, superstar. I was actually hoping to see Karl Litschi win the Pursuit, but all anyone could talk about was this young boy who had come along with a ridiculous bicycle one day and was riding like he had an engine in his belly. I fought my way to the front and what did I see? Karl Litschi, flashing past but looking over his shoulder, turning back to see this young boy who was gaining on him with every pedal stroke. You were catching him.

Ferdy Kübler, who else. You always turn up at the end.

I rode home after that day, telling myself to be more Ferdy. I'd save newspaper clippings whenever they wrote about you, I'd lap up every race report that showed how hard you raced before how hard you fell. You were the boy we all wanted to be.

And then I stopped being Ferdy and I just wanted to beat Ferdy. I used to wait outside Leo Amberg's bike shop and ogle the steel machines through the window until he let me in and he told me to stop this Ferdy nonsense, to be more Hugo. He took me out on his famous training rides and then he took me to the Oerlikon, your Oerlikon, and told the boys there to take it easy on me while I lapped them for fun and they sweated and cursed and I thought to myself, Ferdy Kübler – you're next.

I learned to be more Hugo. Leo sent me off to learn my trade on the track, build my muscles and develop my own style and strength and then you came along, Ferdy Nationale, and I knew that I had to go wherever you went, to win wherever you won because if I could beat you, then I could beat everyone. You probably don't remember it now, but when we first raced on the track, I had you breathing fire.

Back then, I always felt that tomorrow would be better than today. That I'd be faster tomorrow, not because I would have to work particularly hard, but because these things just happened to me. I knew that I could win races and those I couldn't win this year, I'd win them next year. And if I won by ten seconds this year, I'd win by twenty the next. Everything would always get better. I could spend money because tomorrow, there would always be more, and the day after there would be even more. Just turn the taps and watch it all flow.

Someone once gave me a million lira just for a comb. Imagine that, Ferdy.

The curve tilted forever upwards until Mexico, that stupid Tour and those stupid parties. Nobody ever told me that life doesn't keep getting easier, that at some point you reach the top of the curve and you fall, clutching at every last opportunity you can get with both hands until you hit the bottom, without a plan. And then you sit there, forgotten by all but a few, a discarded former racer who doesn't have the legs anymore.

So before you say it, yes, I am an idiot. I've lost everything. The money, my wife, my friends. Except you, Ferdy.

You remember my last race? It was only five years ago and to think I've fallen ever further since then. I was doped, you won't be surprised to learn that, not to win but just to stay upright, hoping that I could show the crowd one final time what it's like to see the great Hugo Koblet race a bicycle and what did I give them? A drugged-up has-been who dragged himself around a velodrome for money he doesn't deserve and that he's unlikely to hold on to. And you were there, by my side, in your cheap suit and your brylcream, and you told me you'd always be there, that I should just enjoy the ride, enjoy the crowds one final time. I enjoyed neither, and I doubt the crowd enjoyed it. But you put on a show and you slapped me on the back and embraced me and told me it's all over, that the next phase of my life is just beginning.

I went home and I cried all night, probably all week, because if Hugo Koblet isn't riding a bicycle, then what is he? What am I? I'm no businessman. My name has no value. The next phase, indeed, Ferdy. What next phase is this? When is it meant to start?

I knew then that the public were forgetting who I was, what I had won. By that time, I had spent more time losing and falling down mountains than I had winning races; only the old men could remember the Hugo that I used to be. Children would look at me, with my receding hairline and my wooden-spoon prizes and they'd actually be looking straight through me, hoping to see someone like Anquetil instead although God knows he's hardly any different from the rest of us, just younger. He'll lose his looks too.

The next phase.

There was no next phase. I hadn't planned for a next phase. I thought my name would suffice, until *the day I realised nobody knew my name.*

Ferdy, I became past tense at the Hallenstadion that evening. I slipped from present to past in the unclipping of a toeclip, and I sank further than I'd ever sank before. Sonja left me, the bills filled the void she left behind and I've been living in a bedsit above a petrol station where I give fuel away free of charge to people I used to know because I'm weak and they pretend to have forgotten their wallets, and I pretend not to mind, pretend not to see the wallet sat there on the passenger seat, and then they drive away never to remember.

And if I'm no longer the Hugo everyone knew, or the Hugo I used to be, what am I? If people look through me, should I really be here? I took the Alfa and I wound the windows down and I felt the air on my face for what I was sure would be the last time. I drove as far as I dared and I turned back, and then turned again, and I found courage for the final time.

Ferdy, even the past tense is forgetting about me. I'm past historic.

ON THE ROAD
AUGUST 1947

The summer of 1947 has gone on too long. Life in Zürich has slowed to walking pace, the city has emptied as it used to before the war years. The heat should relent soon, or so they say. Not long until the first flake of snow and then, all being well, we'll have the warm certainty of indoors and we'll take the family up the mountains. Hot chocolate. Cross-country-skiing. Toboggans. We'll perhaps miss this heatwave. Probably, we won't.

The roads are closed today. Swarms of people are pouring out of the tributary streets of the wide boulevards, all heading in one direction. With crowds comes the warmth – and the personal space – of others. Zürich smells of cigarettes and perspiration. They have come to see a bike race, although in its passage through Zürich this is less of a race, more a procession. The race proper will start once they leave the city, if they can bear the heat.

They have come to see two men in particular. Two

men who wouldn't normally have graced the city of Zürich with their presence, nor would they have graced the Tour de Suisse with their presence either, but they are here nonetheless: Fausto Coppi and Gino Bartali. The first man, Coppi, is a long-limbed Italian deity. He is known to make grown men cry into their coffee. He is young and talented, although not as young as he was seven years ago when he won the Giro against all odds. He could be the next Binda, the next Girardengo, the next Bartali? Gino Bartali is more rugged and inspires a form of stoic devotion. He wears crosses around his neck and the more devout among the cycling fraternity favour him over his supposedly less pious rival. They ignore his 40-a-day cigarette habit and his late-night drinking sessions.

Peep over shoulders and you can see them, if you're lucky. Men have been preparing cameras for weeks on the off-chance they might catch a glimpse of Coppi or Bartali. Children have been telling their friends that they'll get Fausto's autograph, or a polite nod from Gino.

So why are they here? After all, this race – the Tour de Suisse – is usually more of a local affair. A parish race compared to the more established Tours such as the Tour de France and the Giro d'Italia. There are no Grand Tours left this year, so why take part in what is essentially a Swiss race for Swiss riders? Some say they came for the roads – comparatively smooth and untouched by war. Who wouldn't want the smooth hum of concrete under their wheel and the near certainty of a full stage without having to replace your inner tubes five times because the rubble and bomb craters of France and Italy keep shredding your tyres to bits.

Others suggest they more likely came for the favourable exchange rate. Riders are making up for lost time, and lost time is lost money.

And just where did the prize money come from? This may be Switzerland but not everyone here is awash with money. Those in cycling circles may wonder – and many do so vocally in the local press – whether this money may have been better spent developing youth programmes, given the paucity of young Swiss riders entering the professional ranks this year. Just three riders have graduated to professional status this year.

Three.

Those three young riders have the honour of lining up here in the sweaty streets of Zürich alongside the pre-war legends Coppi and Bartali, as well as local legend and former winner of the Tour de Suisse itself, Ferdinand or 'Ferdy' Kübler.

One is a stringbean boy called Hugo Koblet. More of a *pistard* - a track rider - this one. He blows too soon. Another, Fritz Schär, is half the height of Koblet and would appear to be the runt of the litter. Appearances can be deceptive, the boy Schär is tenacious.

All eyes, however, are on Charly Guyot, the son of former national champion Charles Guyot. Charly is a natural, a boy born to the road, a boy so talented that – whisper it – he may be the Swiss Coppi.

There is a story about Charly Guyot. Whether it is true or not, few can say, but it adds to his growing legend. They say that as an amateur, Charly Guyot overslept, missing the start of a race. His opponents looked around, searching for Guyot in vain and could scarcely believe their luck. They left on the dot, relaying furiously, leading each other in slipstreams so as to pool their efforts and achieve speeds that one man alone, in theory, could never reach. They laughed as they rode, making deals. I'll give you 20% if you let me win. I just want a podium place. I'll help you if you give me 30% of your winnings. Let me draft you, I have 20 francs in my pocket.

But there can be no deals with Charly Guyot in attendance. He reached the start line ten minutes late, caught the other riders at the halfway point and was showered and changed before the bedraggled peloton could reach the finish line. That's how good Charly Guyot is. He makes other riders miserable.

The trouble with Charly Guyot is that he really doesn't care much for cycling. He only rides because his father makes him do it. While other kids were racing around town squares for matchsticks and marbles, Charly the younger was on rollers in his father's backyard. The boy has been born into a cycling family, the boy will ride. The boy will be Swiss Champion, just like his father.

The boy will rebel.

Charly dreams of accountancy. Of balance sheets and reconciled payments. A less exciting life, perhaps, but one of comfort, free of injury. And yet his accountancy days are still ahead of him. Here he is, on the start line, filling his father's heart with pride at the sight of his boy alongside Fausto Coppi, Gino Bartali and the rest of them. But Charly doesn't care about Coppi or Bartali, and he doesn't care about the 72 other riders alongside him.

There is one rider alongside the Italians who is overjoyed at their presence. Ferdy Kübler has won this race before although he is plagued with doubt about the worth or the validity of his victory. At the time, Fausto Coppi was a prisoner of war, while nobody knows what Gino Bartali was doing but it must have been heroic for what else would Gino Bartali have been doing? While the rest of Europe was on fire, Ferdy Kübler was beating whoever would turn up. Now 27, Kübler is like many riders of his age – keen to get on with everything at a ridiculous pace, to make up for lost time.

Of course, he was meant to make up for lost time in 1946. That was before the accident-prone rider found himself on the thick end of two crashes, one that broke his collarbone and another that broke too many bones to mention, landing him in hospital for three weeks and ending his season prematurely. Doctors suggested he swap the life of a cyclist for a quiet one. One went so far as to suggest he never ride a bike again.

So as Ferdy lay convalescent at his home in Adliswil, his Cilo team quietly slipped away hoping he wouldn't hear them depart. Nobody called, nobody came. Dr Jan – Cilo's owner – refused to visit

Ferdy in hospital, chalking him up as another bag of broken bones to be discarded, contract unfulfilled. Worst of all, Dr Jan refused to pay the 3,000-franc bill that Ferdy had run up for his three-week stay in hospital.

Well, if the boy's never going to ride again, why bother.

Ferdy spent 1946 sinking further into debt, retreating back into the poverty from which he came.

He had grown up in the border down of Marthalen, a sort of nowhere place in the foothills to the south of Germany. His drunken, badly paid father would work day and night at the asylum over the river, putting potatoes on the table and occasionally the odd sausage to be roast and split between the children. Life at the Küblers was hard, beatings routine. Mothers were known to warn their children that if they misbehaved, they would be sent to the Kübler household as punishment.

Alfred Kübler's presence was bigger than the man himself. A cloud followed him, locals kept out of his way. They say that he broke the day his daughter died and he followed her tiny coffin through the streets of Marthalen. They say he was a gentler man before that. Then he started working at the asylum. That place leaves a mark on a man, and it doesn't pay, either. So Alfred Kübler tinkered and repaired things for people around town.

Ironically – given that he despised bicycles – most of his odd jobs involved fixing them.

It is no speculation that Alfred Kübler hated the bicycle. Many fathers of young riders were fearful of the effect these machines would have on their boys. Not everyone could have a doting father like Charles Guyot. The boy Ferdinand would scoop up newspaper cuttings of heroes such as Georges Speicher and the Maes brothers, little sepia scraps that he would keep in a journal under his mattress. Alfred Kübler tore it to shreds in a fury, then turned his attention to Ferdy's bicycle itself, sawing it in half while his distraught son picked up the cuttings from the bedroom floor.

Ferdy rebuilt a bicycle from bits and pieces he could find lying around. It wasn't pretty, but it moved, and it was a means to an end, the end being distancing himself from his abusive father for as long as possible. He would ride 35km into neighbouring towns to look for work, leaving before the family awoke and returning home as they were putting to their beds.

His first job was for a bakery a full hour's bike ride away. Rising at 5am for a 7am start, Ferdy would attack the bike over the hills and down the lanes that led him to the Pfannenstiel, atop of which the well-heeled residents were awaiting their baguettes and pastries. Young Ferdy would be laden with several kilos' worth of bread, pastry, cake and tart, developing a riding style that would be his and his alone for an entire career. The Pfannenstiel is a relentless climb of curves and hairpins, cambers and potholes. Over the weeks and months that Ferdy served at the bakery, he learned to climb but it took him longer to perfect the art of descending.

Liberated from baked goods, Ferdy spent perhaps more time in ditches than on the road.

Over time, he would graduate from bakeries to jewellers, and it was only a matter of time before someone suggested Ferdy race for real. When he made his amateur debut, the other riders weren't sure what to mock first – his large nose, his ramshackle machine or his baggy clothes. To show them he was serious, he attacked from the off, earning a reprimand from a wide-shouldered local rider called Hug. Hug needn't have bothered as Ferdy's attack fizzled out, establishing a pattern that would persist for many years – suicidal attacks, nervous energy, wave after wave of furious pedalling. Heart rules head.

War arrived before Ferdy could turn professional. Switzerland was surrounded by its enemies and Ferdy was sent up to the mountains as part of Operation Redoubt. Without his bicycle however, he became restless and a fellow conscript informed him that he would be relieved of mountain duties for training if he claimed his professional licence. Even better, he would be able to participate in the Swiss National Pursuit Championships which had been delayed due to the activity on the border. A little fortune, at last.

There was one small problem. Ferdy didn't own a track bike. So he did what any Zürich cyclist would do at that time: he visited Gusti Grabs. Gusti was a tinkerer. He knew people who knew people, just not necessarily the right people, and he had frames and handlebars, just not necessarily matching ones. Gusti helped Ferdy build a bike from bits and pieces they could scrabble together and Ferdy was ready. The professionals now took their turn to mock the big-nosed country boy with floppy hair and floppy clothes. Walter Diggelmann, holder of the title, made a point of pointing at the neo-pro and screaming – look at the country bumpkin – before getting roundly thrashed by Kübler in the quarter finals, caught after just 8 laps of the concrete Oerlikon velodrome.

Robert Zimmerman, winner of the 1939 edition of the Tour de Suisse, was taken apart in the semi-finals in similarly quick fashion before the legendary Karl Litschi was caught in the final and Ferdy – that country bumpkin in the flapping white shirt – because Swiss Pursuit Champion for the first time and everyone knew his name.

In normal times, that would have been the start of something wonderful for Ferdy Kübler. A blossoming career, the opportunity to race Grand Tours in France and Italy and perhaps win them and then earn money trading his name on the track circuit around Europe. All of this was taken away, so Ferdy feels it churlish to complain about his stolen career when other riders were risking their lives fighting for their countries. The presence of Fausto and Gino further reminds him of their hardships while he spent a year suspended from racing due to a dispute over bonus money of all things. You can hardly compare.

When the peloton exited the furnace of Zürich city centre in search of cooler surroundings, Ferdy soon found himself at the front of the race alongside just one of the celebrating pairing – Coppi – and two new faces, Hugo Koblet and Fritz Schär. The quartet worked together, urged on by the Italian, putting distance between themselves and Gino Bartali who was languishing in the pack, unable to respond to each frenzied attack.

Bartali's team car was nervously edging its way alongside riders, team manager Bruno Mariani leaning out to find his man. *Ma dai, Gino, dai! Cosa succede?* Encouragement, shame, confusion – Mariani was trying it all but Gino Bartali was sliding back through lesser riders as if someone had tied lead weights to his rims.

The quartet had extended their advantage over the peloton by several minutes, sweeping through valleys, colourful flashes among the flower-flecked fields. The faster you go, the cooler it gets, so never slow down, never relent, put the knife in Gino's back and twist.

Only with 10km to go did Coppi agree to ease the pace; as the riders crested the final climb ahead of Siebnen, Hugo Koblet attacked his breakaway companions and sprinted into town, crossing the line a full minute ahead of Kübler, Coppi and Schär. It wasn't that they couldn't go with Koblet, just that he wasn't viewed as a threat. But Koblet's elegant and effortless attack was a warning to them all. They just didn't know it.

What they also didn't know was that when Hugo did cross the line, he was disappointed. Disappointed that he wouldn't be wearing the leader's jersey into the second part of the stage. That award would only be granted at the end of the day, once all three thirds of the first stage were complete.

For Ferdy, however, it was far from a disappointment. Having spent the best part of the previous year in bed and having ridden himself into peak fitness over the summer, he rode all morning with a man many considered to be as good as, if not better than Girardengo or Binda. A young boy had got away, but he was a track rider and no serious threat to us road boys. Even better, Ferdy had put three minutes into Gino Bartali, a deficit so serious that Bruno Mariani saw fit to replace Gino as team leader with Giuliano Bresci. An insult.

Insult or tactical masterstroke? As the day unfolded in its unusual three-part stage, Bartali grew into it. The old legs loosened and those three minutes in the morning were found and soon scattered to the hills. By evening, Bartali was in yellow, riding into Davos as if it were his and his alone. Only Constantine Ockers could come within a minute of Bartali, Coppi cracking in the foothills, his energy expended in the heat of the morning.

The next day, Bartali put four minutes into Coppi and five into Ferdy, and the Tour de Suisse was effectively over, just two days into the nine. For Ferdy Kübler though, the press cuttings were yet to be printed.

FERDY: My memories of bike racing are just fragments now, little shards of something I once did unrelated to time and place, just feelings, emotions and sensations that tend to blur into one. Although I do remember the first time we rode together. It was that Tour de Suisse when Gino rode us all into the dirt. I saw you on the first morning and I marvelled at how easy you made pedalling look. I always knew I looked uneasy on the bicycle and I thought – my word, here's my mirror image! My diametrical opposite!

Oh, but there are some stages which are whole memories in themselves. It was two days later, the stage from Bellinzone to Sion, that was where everything changed. I felt all the wrongs of the previous year slot in line behind me. It was the first time I truly felt that I had become a road racer, that I could achieve anything I wanted. I remember so little of the actual riding, fragments of memory that I rearrange as I please, sometimes the result is different. Now and then, I'll take one of those races in which you flew and I'll puncture your tyre – God knows you punctured enough of them yourself – and I'd freewheel past you.

But that stage into Sion, so many of those fragments come from this stage.

I'd take that moment when I looked down the Furka and I saw Gino and Fausto together, chasing me up the hairpins. I'll take that any day. At times, I wonder, did it really happen? Did I, the young Ferdy, go so hard that Gino and Fausto worked together to try to catch me? I marvel at such memories, the audacity of them. How dare I go so far. This was when they weren't even talking to each other, Hugo. I can't remember what had happened that year, one of their many arguments no doubt. They kept several men between them at the start line. I took the pain coarsing through my legs and I remember how quickly it folded away when I realised those sworn enemies were collaborating.

Pain is one of those memories that seems to span my whole career. There is specific pain. Oh, the Ventoux, yes, that was a very specific kind of pain, even if I remember little of the pedalling, little of the actual detail. But that general pain of racing a bike for too many hours, of stretching muscles you thought might snap if you take one more revolution, of having your skin ripped off by the travelling road... all of that pain is one sacred memory that may or may not have happened at a particular moment in time, but I do remember how pain dissipated with urgency and how it returned with boredom.

I take the memory of Rösli, sweet Rösli, waiting for me at the top of that climb. She had brought pineapple slices which I sucked dry in seconds.

Every slice I have ever had since brings back that fragment of memory. She was often there, my dama bianca, with refreshments and a smile and words of encouragement. We had met when I was nursing one of my many cyclocross injuries, she had only known me as an invalid, but to say to her, Rösli – I have climbed the Furka and the two Italians are still many hairpins back. We can take a moment. I'll take that memory and scatter it across all of the races of my life. I see Rösli on the Izoard when Bobet was on one of his good days. I see Rösli on the Stelvio when Fausto had taken la Bomba and had detonated an entire race. Wherever I ride, I see Rösli.

I take the hurt and the boredom of the flat final 100km, and I remember nothing of the landscape, nothing of the arguments between team directors and race organisers. I feel the parched insides of my mouth every time I think of Sion and I feel the hollowed-out emptiness of that lonely run-in every time the wind blows. I felt it in every race after that, I thought of Sion, I thought of how numbing it can be to ride a bike all day, face in the wind, men made of cuts and bruises. This sick, twisted, beautiful sport that made us who we are. I remember that slow ticking down of kilometres, the constant nagging fear that someone is reeling you in, the knowledge that if you turn your head you'll see them or worse, imagine them into being and then you've lost because they've always got the turn of speed you don't have. Sion, every time. I remember the salt from the tears seeping into my wounds and the pain, the searing pain – that's Sion, every time. I remember it from every race, it could have been the Ardennes for all I know, but every time I think of pain I think of Sion and how it was all worth it in the end.

I remember most of all my arrogance that day, though. Oh Hugo, I look back on that day with such shame. The precise words I used, thank God, are lost – recordings cast to the wind, nothing left for posterity other than the shame that I spoke with such a lack of humility that afternoon. What came over me? I remember the microphone – thrust under my nose the second I stopped my bike. Words just fell from my mouth. Only one man could beat Gino Bartali and Fausto Coppi, and that man is Ferdy! Oh Hugo, what an idiot I was. I said something about teaching them a lesson. Nobody teaches Gino Bartali a lesson. I felt like a schoolboy that day, never have I been so stupid. Oh Ferdy, why did you open your mouth? Gino heard about it, he saw me in the hotel corridor that evening and the look he gave me! The next day at breakfast, they were all giving me signs, and sure enough, Gino found me and then he dropped me. But worse, do you know what he did next? He dropped back, dropped me again, dropped back, dropped me again, and kept toying with me like a cat with a dead mouse.

But most of all, I know that as the first time we rode together. The first of the rides of our lives; you were so young, I was so stupid. I had no idea that you'd be the reason I kept riding, the reason I rode so hard until the Ventoux killed me off.

And I look at you now, Hugo. What would we be without each other? What have you done to yourself? If there's no Hugo Koblet, what becomes of Ferdy Kübler?

EPPSTEIN

A small community of cyclists had sprung up in late 1930s Zürich, congregating mostly at the tobacconist kiosk on Militärstrasse, owned and manned by professional rider Fritz Wagner. It wasn't unusual for group rides to start from Wagner's kiosk or for younger riders to hang around flicking casually through newspapers hoping to catch a glimpse of one of the city's top riders such as Walter Diggelmann or Ernst Naef. Diggelmann would enjoy holding court, enjoying the attention of youngsters lapping up his tall tales. Naef was a show-off, capable of eating an entire pack of ten teacakes before tackling a rapid 100km in and out of town.

No more than 200 metres away on the Zwinglistrasse, you would find Herr Eppstein's Jewish boulangerie, famous for its unleavened bread. The owner's son, Paul, would nip out and leave the shop unattended for hours to mooch around outside Wagner's kiosk, hanging onto every word of any cyclist who would let him. Occasionally, he'd be invited out to rides with the local club, the RVZ (Radfahrer Verein Zürich) – and usually he'd find himself struggling to keep up with the pace, even within the city limits before the hard riding actually started. Usually, he'd see their backs riding off into the distance and he'd make a wave as if to say – "have a good ride boys" – and then he'd do a u-turn and head back to the kiosk to see who else was hanging around. Paul's frustration at not being a particularly quick bike rider did nothing to nullify his love of the sport. Instead, he turned his attention to supporting other riders.

At the time, the best bike riders came with their own entourage – mechanics, *soigneurs*, and so on. To be a *soigneur*, you required a licence, and this effectively made you a rider's manager. Paul sought Fritz Wagner's advice on how to procure such a licence and was pointed in the direction of Edi Baumann, a former Olympian who could teach him the art of the *soigneur*. Edi then pointed Paul in the direction of an institute in Geneva where Paul developed further knowledge of the human body and sports performance. He learned about nutrition, mental health, finances – in short, all the component parts of a successful bike rider.

Eppstein found purpose, and soon found a willing clientele. Walter Diggelmann, champion in so many spheres and kiosk braggart, was among the first to take up his services, later referring to Eppstein as "the single best masseur I've ever known". For 1.50, you could have your legs massaged, and for just 50 centimes more you'd get the full hour-and-a-half head-to-toe massage. What's not to like? Fritz Wagner would send riders to Eppstein, including one dishevelled-looking young man who required special attention. Ferdinand Kübler.

This one, Wagner confided, leaning over his kiosk, he's a special case. You'll see. He has the build of a cyclist, his muscles are perfectly formed. He's determined, too – he spent an entire summer in Lucerne as a mechanic, working free of charge in exchange for boarding. Why do you think he did this? Because he wanted to understand how to build the perfect machine. Trouble is, Wagner continued, he needs direction. He doesn't think like a racer should think. He's hot-headed, impulsive. Goes off like a train. He rode in a criterium at the weekend, what on earth possessed him I do not know, but he nearly collapsed 10km from the end. He needs someone to be his brain. Paul, that could be you.

Paul and Ferdy quickly became a team. Paul brought vitamins, improved Ferdy's meagre diet and offered tactical advice which Ferdy often appeared to take on board but usually forgot on the start line. There would be no salary; Ferdy couldn't afford so much as a roast sausage, but both agreed that when Ferdy did win – and both were confident he eventually would – Paul would be rewarded handsomely.

An entourage spun off the kiosk around Paul and Ferdy. Whenever Ferdy won a race, parties would be organised. Eppstein would lead the dance to Hans

Martin's accordion. Ferdy would rise after a couple of songs and tentatively move his feet, to uproarious laughter from the other riders. Hop, Ferdy, Hop, they would shout while the nimbler Eppstein danced lithely around the room, around his less mobile rider. The nights would be long.

The next day they would be climbing the Grimsel and the Furka, Eppstein encouraging his men by telling them that they'd be sleeping in a barn if they couldn't make it to the top by 5pm. Frequently, they were forced to sleep on beds of straw before completing the ride the next morning. On one of those such mornings, Ferdy told his fellow riders that he'd show them all how he's going to win the Tour de France, descending the hairpins of the Furka at a death-defying pace before later being swallowed by the group, struggling to keep up for the rest of the ride. Upon their return, Eppstein would organise parties and music and laughter and Ferdy had never lived a life as full as this.

The problem for both men – in differing respects – lay over the borders. To the north, Germany had already become Greater Germany and was looking southward with disdain and territorial envy. Germany gave reassurances that it would respect Swiss neutrality, but nobody really believed the Germans anymore. To the south, the Italians were viewed as less of a threat, but this was Mussolini. As if he could be trusted. Swiss 'passivity' did not imply that life could simply carry on like this forever.

Ferdy was conscripted in 1939 for the first time. He

presented himself as an athlete, a solid dependable boy. The captain took one look at Ferdy and snorted. What kind of athlete are you boy? A cyclist, he replied, and a very good one at that. I'll turn pro one day. The captain hated cyclists and sent Ferdy up to the mountains as part of Operation Redoubt.

Redoubt was designed to be an overt show of strength to the Germans and the Italians. Invade us and you'll be obliterated.

The Germans certainly were of a mind to invade, and would have done so where they not distracted on different fronts. To Adolf Hitler, those pesky Swiss Germans were a wayward branch of the *Deutsche Volk*. They might as well be French.

And yet even with their mountain fortifications, the risk of invasion from either the north or the south remained ever-present.

Ferdy spent several months in the mountains unable to ride his bike until a fellow conscript asked him why on earth he hadn't procured a professional licence. All the professional athletes were serving in the city so that they could get easier access to facilities. Within a week, Ferdy had his licence and was transferred back to Zürich so that he could resume his training for the mercifully delayed Swiss Pursuit Championships at the Oerlikon velodrome.

Reunited with Eppstein, Ferdy set about putting a bicycle together and while it wasn't pretty, it held firm. Other riders delighted in pointing out the kitchen-sink nature of Ferdy's bike, not least Walter Diggelmann who knew Ferdy from the kiosk, who led the laughter on the Saturday morning ahead of their quarter final meeting. Diggelmann was the reigning champion, but Ferdy caught him on the eighth lap after just 3km of racing.

For Paul Eppstein, it was all coming true. The promise that his rider would provide him with a living was suddenly becoming a reality. Diggelmann wasn't just beaten, he was pulverised, humiliated, crushed to a pulp. The name Kübler was being hollered around the bars and cafes of Zürich. He might look funny, but he's ours and he's the quickest thing we've ever seen on two wheels.

Next up would be Robert Zimmermann, winner of the 1939 Tour de Suisse. What followed ought to have been a salutary warning to young Eppstein, bringing him down from his cloud. Word had got round that Ferdy was sitting next to Zimmerman in the stands while watching the team Championship race, and that the two had secretly agreed that Zimmermann would win in exchange for 200 francs. Eppstein flew into a rage at Ferdy who admitted taking the bribe, claiming poverty.

Eppstein stood his ground, refusing to even speak to Ferdy until he returned the money.

Whether Ferdy returned the money or not is unknown, but he did beat Robert Zimmermann in that semi-final although not in quite as crushing a style as the defeat of Diggelmann.

The final on Sunday would be Ferdy Kübler versus the legendary Karl Litschi, and Eppstein had a plan. Knowing that the centre of the Oerlikon velodrome would be filled with spectators, Eppstein correctly deduced that for the first time this week, the riders would no longer be able to see each other on the opposite side. The only way of knowing where the other rider might be was for the *soigneur* to stand 5 metres ahead of the line in the case of a 5-metre lead, or 5 metres behind the line for a 5-metre deficit. Eppstein's plan was to sow confusion by reversing the rule, posting himself behind the line when Ferdy was ahead. The Litschi team panicked, and whether this played into Ferdy's ultimate victory or not is moot – Ferdy won, and Paul Eppstein took the credit.

Ferdy was Swiss National Pursuit Champion and Paul was the difference. The two embraced and promised to meet later that evening for the customary celebrations with music and dancing and suchlike, perhaps with Hans Martin and his accordion.

And yet that evening, Paul Eppstein sat alone in the café, nursing his empty espresso cup as he gave Ferdy another ten minutes, and another ten minutes, and perhaps just another ten minutes. But still Ferdy didn't arrive.

Two people had intervened in between the pair's parting at the Oerlikon velodrome and Ferdy's no-show that evening. The first man was the most popular cyclist in all of Switzerland at the time, Paul Egli. He had come with an offer. Join my team and become the rider you were always meant to be. I'll turn you into a Tour de France winner, he promised – I'll turn you into the greatest cyclist the world has ever seen, he over-promised. Or, what went unspoken, stay under my wing while I wind down my own career and eke out a few more victories. Better this than get shown up by a young upstart on a dodgy bicycle like Digg and Zimm.

Either way, Paul Egli recognised that Ferdy was a rider of immense potential.

He just didn't see Paul Eppstein as part of the team.

The second man to intervene that evening was Emil Keller, owner of the city-centre Hallenstadion velodrome. Whereas the Oerlikon was a barren concrete bowl exposed to the conditions and used for major championships, the Hallenstadion was the place for drunks and pimps to mingle, fight and perhaps enjoy some of those world-famous cyclists trying to stay upright on their bikes for the famous six-day races. If the Oerlikon was all about achieving your dreams, the Hallenstadion was all about growing your bank balance.

Keller's warning to Ferdy was simple. You bring a Jew into my velodrome and you're out. For good. Find yourself another manager. And to Eppstein directly, a personal warning: "Little Jew, I'll throw you out of the window."

Switzerland may have been neutral, but it wasn't immune to antisemitism. The Germans couldn't get through Operation Redoubt, but the poison could seep over the border in their place. Paul Eppstein found himself cast aside by an awe-struck and intimidated Ferdy Kübler and never saw so much as a centime from Ferdy in payment. He returned to the kiosk and the 1.50f leg massages – if you don't mind being massaged by a Jew – and it took Ferdy a full five years to return to the boulangerie on Zwinglistrasse to apologise for his behaviour and ask Paul if he didn't mind a clean slate. Paul didn't mind. There would be new riders soon enough. Even Gino Bartali would ask Paul Eppstein to work with him, as well as a young rider who was tearing up the Oerlikon, a certain Hugo Koblet.

Eppstein would always have work, but the pain of what happened that night would always remain with him.

THE STARS OF TRACK AND BATTLEFIELD

Ferdy Kübler and Fausto Coppi were both 20 when they met for the first time at the Oerlikon velodrome. Born two months apart, they were similar in every way other than how they approached bicycle racing. Both had grown up poor, both had discovered that the bicycle was a route out of poverty, and both had worked as delivery boys. So goes the story for almost every man in the modern peloton. However, where Fausto was a natural extension of his machine, Ferdy was an assemblage of mechanical parts – pistons and exhausts and steam-powered contraptions. Take Fausto off the bike and he was as gauche and unseemly as Ferdy on it, as if somebody had cobbled an identikit rider from hazy memory. Put him back on his bicycle and the 20-year-old boy from Novi Ligure suddenly made sense.

It also made sense for the two to be matched at this early stage of their careers. Ferdy had just become Swiss National Pursuit Champion, much to the embarrassment of his elders, and had confirmed his promise with wins in cyclocross, track and road competitions. Fausto Coppi had gone one better, winning the Giro d'Italia in an audacious display of disregard for his elders.

Their careers were taking shape in an uncertain world. Fausto's Giro would be the last Grand Tour for several years and racing opportunities were beginning to dry up. He would only be allowed to race abroad in 'friendly' or neutral countries, restricting him to races in Berlin or Zürich when allowed leave from the Italian army. Ferdy found himself equally restricted, so the visit of Fausto was cathartic. Ticket sales were rapid, newspaper coverage ecstatic. Despite the chill of early December, the Oerlikon would be full, standing room only.

As velodromes go, there are few settings like it in the world. The Oerlikon is a concrete velodrome, a brutalist's dream of cold, grey certainty, dumped from the sky in an otherwise undistinguishable suburb of Zürich, with its church, boulangerie and all. Steep and fearful with high banks of seating, the Oerlikon is not a pretty setting like the Vigorelli at its finest, and its raw, open-air aspect lends itself to attritional racing. This is no place for world records or personal bests – you would save that for Paris or Milan, if you were able to race there. This is a place for grinding your opponent into the asbestos.

Ferdy looked out at the start line, at the bare trees above the stands, the crowds in their winter finest all on their feet and then looked across at his Italian opponent, serene and focused. Ferdy went hard from the off, in search of any form of psychological advantage he could find over his rival. In a pursuit race, the two men start at opposite ends of the long straight, the winner being the man who catches the other. The first laps can be non-events, leg-looseners. Or they can be edgy affairs, both men expending more energy than they had anticipated. This is how Ferdy wanted to play it, knowing that Fausto was a time-triallist and would be carefully dosing his effort, measuring every ounce of energy. The only way to loosen Fausto out of this methodology would be to get into his head.

Ferdy edged ahead, lost his advantage and regained it. From a distance, spectators would usually rely on jersey colours to distinguish between the two men, especially when so high up, but not today. Ferdy's technique gives him away before any colour scheme comes into it. In and out of the saddle, arched back, hands moving rapidly up and down his handlebars, nervous tics and looks around for his opponent. Fausto is the swan of bike racing; few movements above the waistline but long legs below the waistline applying enormous power to the pedals at a phenomenal number of revolutions per minute.

For over 3,000 metres, the distance between the two men remains tantalisingly equal, stretching occasionally and snapping back to its former state like elastic, one man sensing an advantage before seeing it snuffed out like a cigarette, the other desperate to retrieve any losses. And almost in the blink of an eye, as if the mechanics of Ferdy Kübler had discovered a fault, the lights start to go out. Fausto's legs appear to turn ever faster as the hunter discovers his prey limping. Ferdy's legs lose rhythm and turn to percussion, a syncopated struggle with the machine he wrangles. Nothing is right. Everything is wrong.

Watching their boy suffering, the Oerlikon crowd are on their feet, mute. Fausto sees the race through their eyes, a tragedy unfurling in front of them, he the villain, Ferdy the victim. He sees the glory in the defeated hero, the boy who fights, and he sees the fear in the eyes of the Oerlikon faithful, he hears the deafening, frozen silence. Through that silence, he can make out the metallic crunch of each bump in the surface as he closes in on Ferdy. He hears Ferdy's heavy breathing, his squeals of pain and self-encouragement, his cranks relenting under the pressure.

He passes Ferdy after just 3,750m and is informed shortly afterwards that this is his fastest ever pursuit at an average of 50.51km per hour, an extraordinary achievement that he would never match, not at the Oerlikon, not at the Vigorelli, not at any velodrome in the world. Ferdy Kübler had pushed Fausto Coppi as hard as any other rider thus far in his short career and later that afternoon would beat him in a sprint to win the second leg.

An exuberant Fausto embraced his rival, inviting him back to the Vigorelli for a revenge match.

FERDY: *It was in 1942, I was given the honour of finally travelling down to meet Fausto for the revenge match at the Vigorelli. Oh, Hugo, when I met Fausto for the first time at the Oerlikon, it meant everything to me. I knew that day that I wanted to race Fausto every day, and if not against him why not with him. He was so young, he had none of the problems that would come in later years, he just rode his bicycle as if he were floating on a cloud. I'll always remember those words – "Ci vediamo al Vigorelli, Ferdinando!"*

Paul put me to work, made me train day and night. He'd leave me behind on mountain passes and I'd come back an hour later to find him tucking into a chicken leg. How did he get a chicken leg without killing it himself, I don't know. There was never any left for me. He said I'd never catch Fausto if I couldn't catch Paul Egli and then he'd turn the lights out and go to sleep. The next morning, we'd ride another 200km and he'd drop me again. But I learned to manage myself and he entered me into races, some good ones too.

And then the situation turned, as it seemed to do every day. I was sent to Zug to stay inside a school which acted as a barracks, and they banned me from bike racing. All of this just months before I was supposed to meet Fausto in Milan. I tossed and turned in my bed, wondering what on earth to do, how on earth to train. And then one night at 4am, I crept out and went back home, took my bike from its shed and I rode for two hours in my civvies before sneaking back in and slithering back into the cold blankets on those awful straw beds they had. I did this for four weeks, Hugo. Four weeks and I thought not a soul had noticed! But the guards, they knew.

One morning I was told the Colonel wanted to see me. That was it, I thought – I can kiss goodbye to the Vigorelli, I may never see Fausto again.

"Radio Operator Kübler", he bellowed. "I hear that you've been going out in civilian clothes on your bicycle!"

I cursed myself for the indiscretion. What a fool I was, Hugo!

He continued. "So it turns out that you are a professional bicycle racer, Radio Operator Kübler. You do realise that you have committed a crime by sneaking out at night in your civilian clothes?"

My heart sank. So this really was it. The end. I tried to defend myself; I blurted out something crazy like "But I traded sleep for training – it's not like I've been riding during working hours!"

And I remember this so clearly, I'll remember it all my life. He looked at me, and he laughed. He actually laughed at me, Hugo. He said, "Most boys these days are too lazy to take up any sport at all. The fact that you've been out training instead of sleeping is absolutely commendable, young Mr Kübler. I'll give you a vacation so that you can train and travel to Milan, but above all – do not let us down at the Vigorelli!"

On my way out, one of the guards whispered to me – "You got away with that one, Ferdy!"

Paul picked me up and we drove to Milan so that I could practice on the Vigorelli itself. You know, when I first saw that Milanese velodrome, I fell in love with it. How fast you could ride – we always used to love riding on that dark, Californian wood, how it would always give you something extra in the wheels. How the banks were so perfectly formed that you felt no incline on leaving the curve – the most balanced velodrome I've ever ridden, Hugo. And yet you're always afraid, afraid of falling, the fear of splinters, it keeps you upright, it keeps you focused. So many records here, so many legends went before me.

You know of course that Fausto won, but I really didn't mind. I had escaped the barracks for a short while, I had ridden at the Vigorelli while so many others around me could dream of nothing other than an end to the war. But Paul Egli was still angry with me...

When Paul Egli says five o'clock in the morning, he means five o'clock in the morning. Not five to five. Not five past five, and most certainly not quarter past five. He embodies perhaps the most stereotypical of Swiss caricatures, that of the irate timekeeper.

Young Ferdy was late. Paul paced up and down the room before noticing the arched back and ungainly riding style of his pupil coming down the road at high speed. He leaned out of the window and yelled at the top of his voice:

"Fucking brat! If I'm going to teach you one thing, it's to be punctual. I said five o'clock, not quarter past you little shit."

Ferdy had overslept, yes, but had ridden so fast that those fifteen minutes had been cancelled out in no time. Were it not for a level crossing hampering his progress, he'd have made it on time. Not one train but two passed him by, but Paul didn't care.

"Go home. Piss off. I don't want to see you today. Come back tomorrow at 5 o'clock – ON THE FUCKING DOT!"

With tears in his eyes, Ferdy remounted his bike, rode back to his guest house and returned to bed a scolded child. The next morning, he made sure to arrive ten minutes early and Paul didn't say a word about his tantrum the previous day.

Each day, Egli's training schedule took in different mountain passes. In one ride, the Grimsel and the Furka, back down into Zürich. Another day, it was the San Bernardino on the way to Lugano. One morning, Egli noticed Ferdy's light inner tubes and burst into a characteristic fit of rage:

"You can't bring those tubes up to the pass! I tell you what Ferdy, if you go flat, I'm not helping you. You're on your own, you idiot."

As fate decreed, Ferdy did go flat on the San Bernardino. Paul rode past and huffed. "Fix it yourself boy, I'm not helping."

And so Ferdy sat down in the grass, fresh mountain

air whipping around his neck as he fiddled with inner tube, needle and thread. Supply problems meant that every inner tube had to be looked after with great care and preserved for as long as possible. For over an hour, Ferdy sat alone, sewing, sealing, testing and fitting his wheel before finally being able to tentatively climb back on his machine and descend the San Bernardino.

A little later in Lugano, Ferdy found Paul sitting on the terrasse of a restaurant.

"Oh you made it then," he grunted.

"Yes I am, and that was hard work no thanks to you!"

"Well, how on earth are you ever going to learn that professional bike racers look after their equipment? Bring the right equipment for the right races, at all times. I don't care how hard things are."

With Egli's scoldings permanently at the back of his mind, Ferdy prepared in earnest for the 1942 Tour de Suisse by eating three steaks, vegetables, bread and fruit before the start of the first stage, hoping to gain a nutritional advantage over the field. Just a few kilometres out of the start town of Winterthur, Ferdy began to realise that he may have badly interpreted his mentor's advice. The food was weighing Ferdy's stomach down badly, and he watched other riders coast away from him with apparent ease.

When Ferdy arrived at the finish line a full seven minutes after the pack, Egli demanded to know what the hell was going on.

"Well, I took your advice and I ate three steaks,

loads of bread, vegetables, some fruit…"

Egli smacked his head in frustration.

"For the love of God, Ferdy, I didn't say you should eat all of that just before a stage!"

The next day, Ferdy rode on a lighter stomach but it started badly for Egli himself who punctured early on in the stage. His young *domestique de luxe* waited for him before puncturing too while Egli rode away. Ferdy fought hard to get back into the main pack of riders but couldn't find Egli in the group – he had ridden further ahead. So Ferdy sprung from the pack and climbed the San Bernardino at an electric pace, catching up with his leader on the descent.

Egli allowed Ferdy to compete for the stage and catch the day's leader, the Luxembourg rider Matthias Clemens. Clemens would have looked in horror as blackboards were frantically rewritten with his lead cut almost every 30 seconds. Over the space of ten kilometres, Ferdy had reduced his lead from 1'30" to just 20 seconds. When he punctured, he saw Ferdy coming down the road like a train and waved his arms, screaming "I'll give you 500 francs if you stop and help me", but Ferdy pretended not to hear and ploughed ahead to win the stage, while Paul Egli came home to wear the yellow jersey for the first time in his long career.

That evening, as Egli celebrated both his victory and the ill fortune of his age-old rival Leo Amberg who was suffering from stomach cramps, the news came in that the Luxembourg team had lodged a complaint against Egli for drafting their vehicle. Egli conceded that yes, he may have drafted the vehicle for a short moment after having punctured, but on closer study of the rules, he discovered that the penalty for drafting – for any length of time – was relegation to the same time as the man in penultimate place.

Paul Egli had held the yellow jersey for a matter of hours before having to give it up... to Ferdy Kübler.

Devastated, Egli went home, abandoning the Tour and leaving Ferdy to his own devices. Ferdy offered to quit as well, out of solidarity, but Paul told him to shut up and keep racing, wear the yellow jersey for a day or two and consider it training.

Ferdy had no support. Other riders formed alliances with each other. Leo Amberg, desperate not to let one of Paul Egli's men win, teamed up with Hans Martin to help a rider called Fritz Stocker who lay fifth in the General Classification. They tortured poor Ferdy over the next three stages, toying with him and attacking relentlessly. Ferdy was then approached by Karl Litschi, the man he had humiliated at the Oerlikon velodrome several years ago. Litschi asked for 500 francs in exchange for his support. Ferdy agreed, and he brought Ferdy home for what would be his first Tour win.

Karl Litschi never received his 500 francs.

Ferdy had won the Tour de Suisse for the first time, and it would be a landmark victory, if not a spectacular one. He had earned begrudging respect from Paul Egli who, finally, accepted that Ferdy had to come out of his shadow. He had earned the respect of the peloton, in particular for the second stage up the San Bernardino. But as war escalated all around them, the Swiss riders found themselves isolated. Supply lines were being cut off, rationing cards were brought in, and riding a bike, all of a sudden, felt a little frivolous.

The boy at the front of the group of three riders is wearing, for the first time, the white, red and blue jersey of the RVZ cycling club underneath a pink shirt. As he rides through the empty roads of Zürich's Aussersihl district, he strips off his shirt and packs it into a bag that he has taken from his back.

"Still not told your mother, Hugo?" laughs one of the other boys.

"Not a word," laughed the boy, throwing the satchel back over his shoulder. "And don't you dare mention it to her!"

Hugo Koblet is 18 years old. He lives with his doting mother Helena and his less-favoured brother Adolf above the Koblet bakery, and though his mother doesn't yet know it, Hugo is a bike racer. He tells her that he's training to be a mechanic, or that he's working in a factory. Anything to convince her that he won't be risking life and limb throwing himself down mountains or round velodromes on a flimsy metal claptrap.

He is still too thin. Two years ago, his mother was so worried about her rake-thin son that she dragged him by his ears to the doctor. Hugie worries me. Hugie is too thin for a boy his age. He eats, and yet he never grows outwards, just upwards. Look at his beautiful face. This boy needs to fill out. You have to help, doctor, you have to make him stronger.

The doctor's reply was that Hugo needed to spend more time outside. Fresh air will make him stronger, Frau Koblet. With this welcome advice ringing in his ears, Hugie left Zürich for Davos where he would ski, play ice hockey and breathe the purest of pure air. He grew taller, not wider, and his mother called him back to work at the bakery for his brother.

Adolf provided little inspiration for the ambitious Hugo who was put to work sweeping the floor and cleaning windows instead of baking cakes and pastries. He started work for the Belmag factory as an apprentice and even earned a qualification as a silversmith in the process.

Hugo spends half his time in Leo Amberg's bike shop these days, putting a shine on the Amberg bikes and sweeping the floor, anything for a few more moments in Leo Amberg's presence, a few more anecdotes about the Tour de France or the Tour de Suisse. Amberg, for his part, sees in Hugo a rider of some potential. He's told his brother-in-law Hans Martin, he's told anyone that will listen, there's a young boy who comes to the shop, and he'll wipe the floor with the lot of you, just you see.

Leo took Hugo to the Oerlikon, let him ride with

the RVZ boys to get a taste of the track, but they asked him to stop when he went too hard and had them all breathless. Leo told him to come back when he'd learned to respect other riders, and suggested that a time trial might be more his thing. Less embarrassing for everyone else.

"How long Hugo?" shouts the boy at the back.

"Another 5km, if you can handle it?" he replies, before launching into full-on attack mode.

That May morning, the boys of the RVZ were heading to Leo's suggested time trial. It seemed simple enough – 16km, mostly downhill, from Dietikon to Hasenberg. Hans Martin would be there at the start line, especially for Hugo they say, and Leo Amberg would be there at the finish, only for Hugo. The time trial would be downhill, but to reach Dietikon, the only way is up. Hugo leads the way, still, dancing on his pedals in between dew-soaked banks of grass, his friends breathless in their attempts to keep up.

When they arrive, Hans Martin fusses around Hugo, reprimanding him for exerting himself excessively on the climb to the start line, checking his bicycle, his brakes, his tyres. The other boys barely get a look in.

When Hugo departs from the start line, silence falls. Their work is done, and if Hugo is as good as Leo says he is, then we might as well all go home.

For Hugo, cycling is easy. This is his first time trial, and yet his legs turn as if he's been doing this since birth. He sees riders ahead of him, getting closer with each pedal stroke, and he passes them with a gentlemanly wave and an encouragement. For other riders, the humiliation of being surpassed by this boy, this whippet-thin child, is compounded by his sincerity, his humility. Did he actually apologise as he flew past?

Winning the time trial is not a surprise to Hugo, nor is it a surprise to Leo Amberg who crouches, tiger-like, at the finish line, stopwatch in hand. While Hugo wonders how to tell his mother, how to conceal the trophy and the flowers and the side of ham that will be awarded to him, he wonders also – how is it that Leo Amberg, the greatest cyclist in all of Switzerland, is timing me, today, at an amateur time trial?

Could I really be that good?

THE LONG ROAD HOME FOR LEO AMBERG

Leo Amberg had denied it for too long, but it was now time to accept the inevitable. His career was over. As he sat, watching the road stretch away from him between the canvas flaps of an old army van, he thought of ways to trick his body into riding one more year. One more Tour. But that was the problem. It would require some form of magic to get another year out of these legs.

What then am I, he would ask himself. What am I if I cannot trick these legs into turning the pedals?

Leo owned a bike shop in Zürich. He would never be short of work and with his new frames, he'd have a production line, cashflow, sales – all being well. There's money in making bikes. Just not as much money as there is in riding them.

The lure of the road still pulled at Leo's heart, though. The lure of those achievements that were denied him, stolen by the war. After all, Leo had finished third in the Tour de France ten years ago in

1937. He was 25 then. A young man standing on the precipice of a glittering career. He'd make a fortune riding criteriums, the track would keep him through the winter. But the road... it was always about the road.

He let people believe that he'd been coaxed into this year's Tour, the first since the war ended. There had been *kermesse* races around churches and town squares in France, a couple of criterium races too, enough to rouse those legs in preparation. Amberg is still a name people remember, organisers pay a handsome sum for the man who came third in the Tour of '37.

But *le Tour?* Oh, the Tour. Well, if you really think so... I could be persuaded...

Leo was named road captain of the Swiss National Team by Heiri Suter, a role that befitted his veteran status, a role that implied seniority. In reality, it was a role that involved getting Ferdy Kübler – the team's cash cow – into the best position for stage wins and, ultimately, financial reward.

Leo would have to swallow his pride. Ferdy was Paul Egli's man. Leo despised Egli and made sure everyone knew about it. He'd refer to him as 'that bastard Egli' and would ride against any of Egli's boys just to make sure there was never an Egli rider on the podium. It also helped bike sales, to have a rival. A great rivalry pays its way in column inches, and column inches pay their way in bike sales. The name Amberg lives on.

The '47 Tour had begun in Paris under burning skies. Stay motionless for more than an instant and you'd feel a searing pain across your skin. So you move and you move fast, you are the breeze that cools you down. Leo rode on the front that day, keeping Ferdy safe, keeping Ferdy in position for the sprint into Lille. He sought space where it could be found, threading a line through the wheels, hollering instruction, stay close – wait for my call – we're going left. Leo had consumed the road book, digested its every page, he knew just when to wait and when to attack. Now, Ferdy, go! And Leo would drop back, conveniently harming someone else's sprint, not a word of apology. The yellow jersey was theirs, and with it the cagnotte, the jackpot, the stage winnings and the column inches. Amberg the name, Amberg the bike.

The second stage saw Ferdy doing what Ferdy does best. Attacking relentlessly from the start and blowing up 50km from the finish. Leo should have seen it coming. The madman on a bike cannot be kept in check for more than a day. Ferdy dropped out of the peloton, spat out like a discarded toy from a pram, Leo the forlorn parent having to retreat. 14 minutes, they lost. 14 minutes behind Tour favourite René Vietto. Ferdy threw his bike into a field and sat beneath a tree, crying his eyes out. Leo left him for a while, not quite knowing what to do, before plucking up the courage to wrap his arm around Ferdy's shoulder and mutter words of sympathy. There, there. We always have tomorrow.

A puncture the next day – more or less on the border between Belgium and France – found Ferdy under further pressure. Leo stuck by his man, repairing the puncture himself, keeping calm and holding a smile throughout. A joke or two, to distract Ferdy from the calamity that was unfolding. Keep your head down now, Ferdy, ride and we'll catch them before long.

The trouble was that they were so far behind, those manning the feeding station had long since packed up and gone home. And so they raced to the second station only to find they were so late that the tables had been folded up and all that was left were scraps of food lying by the roadside. Crowds had gone home, too, so Leo went knocking on doors, shouting at windows. Some food, something to eat, we're riders in the Tour de France and we're late. Hungry. Starving.

All he could find was a slice of cheese so old that the rind had invaded, taken over.

"Is that the best you can do," sneered Ferdy.

Leo cocked his head to one side and retorted: "Tell you what, pull up a table, stick a napkin in your jersey and I'll cut it up into little pieces for you."

Ferdy laughed and ate the cheese.

They rode on, joined by their teammate Tarchini and finished last, over an hour and a half behind the winner but mercifully within the time limit outside of which they would have been expelled from the Tour.

The night in Luxembourg would be one of the

warmest of the heatwave thus far. Leo soaked the bedsheets in cold water for Ferdy, insisting he sleep on top, but Ferdy barely slept. He tossed and turned, one eye on the clock, wondering how the hell he could ride a 250km stage the next day. Announcing his decision to withdraw from the race at the breakfast table, Ferdy was met with laughter, a sizeable meal and Leo's renowned good humour. It wasn't long before Ferdy had forgotten his early retirement and was back on the bicycle.

Ferdy wasn't alone in having a sleepless night, so the pace had slowed noticeably. The stage from Luxembourg to Strasbourg was the collective effort of a peloton worn down by the heat. One man could be heard above the grumbling, cracking jokes and telling anecdotes to the men around him, pushing his protected rider up the most minor of climbs – Leo Amberg – the man who came third ten years ago, the man who's looking after Ferdy Kübler.

40km from the finish, the Breton rider Jean Robic decided enough was enough and broke from the stupor of the peloton, joined by another French rider, Maurice Diot. Leo Amberg looked up from his handlebars after a momentary lapse and saw someone was missing. He looked behind, looked to both sides – where the hell had Ferdy gone?

He's gone with Robic, came a voice. Your job's done Leo!

Ferdy had indeed followed Robic's attack and when Maurice Diot slowed down to grab a beer extended to him from an arm in the crowd, Robic and Kübler attacked again, leaving Diot to rue his thirst alone. The two attacked the streets of Strasbourg, only for Ferdy to puncture and fall on a corner. Robic took the win and Ferdy rolled in on his flat tyre to receive warm words and consolation from Carl Senn, President of the Swiss Cycling Federation.

"Go fuck yourself, Senn", muttered Ferdy, leaving his punctured yellow bike on the pavement.

As temperatures cooled slightly, Ferdy took advantage of Leo Amberg's slipstream once more to win the stage into Besançon. Leo's plan to slingshot his rider in for as much money as possible was paying off.

The Alps were rising into view, and Leo unveiled his plan to ride on wooden rims that he had had built specifically for the mountains. Amberg rims, he grinned. While Lyon to Grenoble was meant to be a transition stage before the climbing began, Leo insisted on using the rims, and urged Ferdy to eat and drink continually, to save himself for the climb of the Galibier the following day. This was after having consumed very little at breakfast, knowing that other riders would be weighed down by the copious offerings at the team hotel. This time, when Leo punctured, it was Ferdy who dropped back to wait for his road captain, even after having chased Jean Robic's attack on the col d'Epine. Better to look after the man who helps him rather than chase down an attack 150km from the finish.

Ferdy and Leo restarted together but found that while the rims were holding, the Simplex derailleurs were not. As the gradient turned negative, they were unable to find the revolutions needed to accelerate down the mountain. Leo knew they were losing time but believed all along that they would make it into Grenoble before the cut-off. There would be no chivvying, no cajoling, just a furious relay into the town centre of Grenoble only to find, when they arrived, the streets swarming with spectators and cars. Leo panicked, at one point getting off his bike and running through the crowds – what time is it? Jesus Christ Ferdy, what the hell time is it?

They finished 67th and 68th, nearly 52 minutes behind the stage winner Jean Robic. Perhaps Ferdy should have chased that attack down after all. The commissaires were still calculating, leaving the two Swiss riders uncertain of their fate until midnight, when they decided that Leo and Ferdy had missed the cut by two minutes and 40 seconds. The only way back into the Tour would be to make a written plea to the organisers.

They wrote their plea, and even prepared as if ready to race, sending their suitcases ahead of them to the finish, but Jacques Goddet stood firm. The cut-off is the cut-off and if you don't make it, you can go home. No exceptions, no written letters, no pleading. And as your suitcases have already gone, you'll have to jump into this army van and follow the back of the race. You can collect your things and leave from there.

The two men looked into the beaten old army wagon, its canvas flaps held back to reveal two bare wooden benches. Ferdy climbed in, found his corner and sat morosely, head in hands, feeling that his career would never start, that he'd never win a Grand Tour, that riding a bike really is just a career after all.

With their Tour over, the Swiss pair followed the peloton for seven hours in excruciating silence. At each stop of the broom wagon for injured or simply over-tired riders, the van would draw to a standstill and wait before slowly pulling away. Leo and Ferdy barely spoke a word throughout that tedious journey over the Galibier, around its hairpins which swayed them from side to side. Occasionally, someone would try to peek a glimpse into the wagon, folding back the flaps, but most were already on their way home, long after the parade had finished.

Leo's career was over. No more trickery. No more magic to find in those tired legs. It was time to go home.

SIX DAYS

Armin von Buren picks his way through the tangled web of legs and bike parts, his new racing partner Hugo Koblet following politely in his wake, apologising to all who he disturbs. The two are new to Antwerp and new to each other; neither are new to their competitors. The best spots in the room have already been reserved. Rik van Steenbergen has his own mattress, touch it at your own risk. The Italians claimed their spots early. All that's left for the two young Swiss riders is a nook under the pipes, next to the radiator. This may or may not be a good thing. Hugo notices the pipe is dripping. Not a good thing, then.

They are in Antwerp for a Six-Day track race, six days of non-stop racing. In the old days, they'd ride alone around the velodrome 24 hours a day. The Americans loved it, the sadists. Crowds would flock to see Major Taylor who famously whipped them up into a fury when he audaciously slept for an hour at night, but he then won them back round when he collapsed in front of 12,000 people, promptly fell asleep on the track and not even the vociferous roars of the crowd could wake him. When he did revive, he climbed back on his bike and finished eighth and everyone loved Major Taylor once more.

After time, organisers agreed that riders could compete in teams of two, one riding while the other caught up with some rest or ate. Riders would alternate throughout the day, slinging each other back into the race so that one could rest while the other sprinted laps. And so on, and so on. At first, the American fans hated it – who wants to see riders recover? What wimps they are. It took a concerted PR effort and notably some handy words in the media from a team doctor who bemoaned that the riders were "on the edge of reason" and that he heartily recommends they stop the practice altogether. Hurrah for that, they shouted, and then flocked back to the velodromes.

Six-day racing was brought over to Europe by eager velodrome owners. They had been to Buffalo and New York and had seen the fervour of the fans. At first, they were tentative; they started with an eight-hour race and called it a Madison, after Madison Square Garden. The French preferred "*a l'américaine*", because it didn't sound quite as American and eventually they plucked up the courage to ask the riders to ride for six days which wasn't hard because most of them had been doing it in America anyway. Venue owners would strike deals with the riders – ride hard all day and we'll neutralise the race once the crowds have gone home in the early morning. Ride in a duvet if you really wish to. Have an hour off so we can sweep up the mess. Some riders would ride the neutralised hours with one foot on the handlebars while the other pedalled as they sipped hot chocolate, or sometimes something stronger.

Hugo and Armin recognised the smells of the Six Dayer as they settled into their corner. The oils, the alcohol, the lingering farts.

They'd asked Armin to look after Hugo, which at first sounded like an imposition – this boy's better than you so we'd like you to look after him. But after just an hour in Hugo's company, Armin knew that he'd ride to the end of the earth for Hugo. And back again. Armin knew his limitations. He used to think that his entire career would be spent at the Hallenstadion in Zürich. He lived not far away, having been born equally not far away; the Hallenstadion would be his office. He was a smart sprinter, an able teammate, and for the organisers, he would provide a great backstory. The local boy come good, here to take on the global superstars and very often beat them. This is Armin's track, come take him on if you dare.

Compared to Hugo, Armin is probity personified. He tells Hugo to cut down on the sausages, to improve his diet and cut down on the spending. This is a career for Armin but for Hugo, it's a lifestyle. Hugo responded by telling Armin that he'll cut down on the sausages if Armin smokes a little less. Armin retreats to the corridor to finish his cigarette.

Hugo looks around the room, scans for faces he knows or at the least, faces he recognises from the papers. Stan Ockers is talking to van Steenbergen, that's a formidable combination. He met Stan on the road, briefly, but never van Steenbergen. Not yet. There are two Dutch riders called Gerrit; they've come with an entourage three times that of Hugo and Armin's. There's one Belgian in the corner with a syringe. Another with a box of pills that he stashes inside a pocket inside another bag inside another bag, as if secrecy is really needed.

How else do you ride for six days, thinks Hugo. How did they use to ride without a break? He marvels at the very idea as if riding in a team of two isn't hard enough already. Every Six Day race takes at least six more days' recovery; that's six days you can't ride to your maximum or indeed shouldn't be riding at all – that's six days without pay. But they pay so well, especially if you can cut deals with other riders. He wonders who to make deals with, how it works on this track – when to ask, how to ask. Do you ask here or on the track? Do you let some riders win the intermediate sprints, take the bonuses and then ask if you can have the next one? Armin will know. That's why they've given me Armin, he thinks. This is what Armin does for a living.

Hugo rides first while Armin reads his book underneath the leaky pipes by the radiator. It's a disorganised cat-and-mouse chase of riders climbing the banks, sprinting for no reason other than to rack up the laps. There's nudges and shoves, a couple of minor falls, and then everything settles down for five minutes while the crowds settle down and rush off to find drinks. An Italian breaks the temporary stupor and everyone follows, darting up and down the banking, colours interchanging as the first changes are made. Armin rides on and Hugo reaches behind, feels out for his teammate and grabs a hold of his jersey, slingshotting him into the race for the first time. One down, thinks Hugo, I don't know how many to go.

Come 6am, the revellers have gone, the cigarette smoke has cleared and the hardy ones, the ones with no homes to go to, perhaps, remain wrapped in shawls sipping hot drinks. A truce is called. The cleaners come on to sweep up the paper cups and fag ends, and the neutralised laps begin shortly after. Blankets are passed round, the temperature drops by the minute. One of the Belgians is riding with one eye shut, slumped over his handlebars. A Frenchman pulls alongside for a chat.

"Vous êtes Suisse, non? Alors, vous parlez Français?"

Hugo does speak French and delights in the company. He asks about the deals, about who's in charge when van Steenbergen is off the track, about whether there's anything to be done at night. No, his French friend insists, you just get through the night together and wait for the crowds to return. Hugo tells his new friend about America, of how the Americans would ride hard for two days to accumulate laps, but once you knew their strategy, you'd get used to it and you could beat them on days five and six when they could barely sit on their saddles any longer. How the Swiss riders were called Watchmakers and Cuckoo Clocks by the other riders, of how the hastily made tracks almost seemed to fall apart by day six. And then it was too late to talk, and Armin was on the track anyway. Armin would ride until midday, by which time the hardcore would have returned and Hugo would race again.

He lay down on his mattress and thought of the money. 5,000 francs for this event. In time, this would rise – he just knew it. Look at Ferdy Kübler; he could get 15,000 because everyone wants to see Ferdy Kübler. The crowds swell at the very mention of his name. Fausto Coppi doesn't come this far north very often, but when he does, he can double Ferdy's wage in a night.

He listens to the conversations around him, at least those he understands. In Hannover, someone says, the velodrome director plonks a chair at the bottom of the track every night, making the riders climb the banks to stay alert. What a bastard, Hugo thinks. What a clever bastard. Another rider was complaining about someone slipping sleeping pills into his coffee. Spiked – can you believe it? Who would do such a thing.

And then Hugo falls asleep, a fitful, short sleep during which all he can see is revolutions of a velodrome, all he can feel is the circular movement of his feet and his legs and the sudden rises and falls of tempo. And then he wakes, staggers forward and finds his bike.

Armin is shouting his name.

DOWN AND OUT
IN BUFFALO

HUGO: *She has blue eyes. Brown hair. My arms around her slim waist. Her scent is honey, or maple syrup, probably from her pinafore which hasn't been washed for days. Such are the times. Her skin is fair, unblemished, her breath like pancakes, her voice brittle and clarinet-hard.*

I see those azure eyes widen, cast themselves to the other end of the room. There is music playing, someone has crashed into the restaurant, making an awful racket. He sounds foreign, he sounds Swiss, he sounds like... oh shit, it's Gopf.

I'm sorry, I say, I don't think I can stay much longer and I break from her before she can insist, but Gopf is on top of me. I land on a table, cutlery goes flying. Gopf's fists are flying. I roll out from under him and run for the door, laughing like an idiot. Gopf grabs my leg and pulls himself up and with one surprise left hook – I never knew he was capable – he connects and I'm back on the floor.

Tick. Tock. Out for the count.

She's not the marrying type, I shout after him as we hit the sidewalk. I am slightly stunned, a little dizzy. She is my type though. She's very much my type, for a night or two, no more. He's such a fucking saint.

Gopf, I shout, come on mate. I was just playing around.

Playing around? Gopf retorts, wild-eyed, his hair sprouting from all angles. Playing around?

Gopf has a habit of repeating himself, as if he needs to hear himself say something twice to believe he's actually said it. He does this on the bike too which makes him incredibly easy to read. Want to know if Gopf is starting his sprint? He'll look round twice to make sure you've noticed.

You were playing around with a waitress, there's nothing new there. But working in a bloody restaurant all night?

Yep, bang to rights.

Gopf, we're broke. We need the money.

We're broke? We're broke?

There he goes again.

I'm done with you, Hugo. Done. You fuck everything up, everywhere you go, you fuck everything up. Think of the man you could be, Hugo. We've got Six Days coming up and where do I find you? Washing dishes and screwing waitresses.

He's not mentioned the drinking, or perhaps he's saving it up for later.

Yes, we do have Six Days coming up, that's six

days on the track, no drinking, no flirting, no hamburgers, just going around and around so that we can earn some money to go drinking, flirting and eating hamburgers. There was Chicago before this, blind drunk in spit and sawdust. New York was more elegant. Jazz all night, women who looked you deep in the eyes as if reaching into your soul. Oh, the dancing, the hair that crackled and whipped you and the lights of so many colours. In Philadelphia, we ate and we rode, urban boys turned country bumpkins at the buffet of life. Gopf approves of the food, disapproves of the drink.

I relent and trudge faithfully behind him, for what can I say? He's right, and I am wrong. We're here to race, not to cause trouble or be troublesome. But America... what is it about this country that makes me want to run wild with abandon and try everything in sight? The food, the drink, the women, the cars, the long, wide open roads, the burgers and the clothes, the hats, the women, the cars, the sights, the cigarettes, the women, the cars... Gopf is a saint and I don't deserve him. He looks at the temptations of this country and stands back – oh Lord, save me from America.

I wake the next day. Gopf has already gone downstairs for breakfast or perhaps he's already left for the velodrome. I shower and think of the waitress with the azure eyes and perhaps I'll see those deep blue eyes piercing into me for an hour or two, urging me to ride harder, to stay upright for one more revolution. We are part of a travelling circus, Gopf and I. Wearing our red jersey and our white cross for the entertainment of others at a pop-up velodrome that tours the country, gradually deteriorating day by day until you hear the creaks and the cracks under your wheels, threatening to fall apart and swallow you up. We race as if in an orchestra, one minute you are the string section, the next you're soloing and then you are percussion, always there but unnoticeable, waiting for the conductor to bring you back. This is racing with structure, with plot, all scripted and purchased in advance, bargains struck, stories written for eager journalists hoping for a Major Taylor to whip the crowds up into a fury. Gopf doesn't get that. Gopf rides because that's all he knows; it pays the bills and whether he wins or not, it doesn't matter.

I ride because I love the spectacle. The whole.

Today, the organisers have asked for a fall. Twisted wheels, broken arms, whatever we can provide. Work it out between yourselves. You do the choreography. Boys who fall will earn double tonight, triple if you can get back on your feet and ride the night. Tomorrow, you can ride safely but do us all a favour and look like ghosts. Look like you're hating it. Wobble a little, pretend you're going to be sick. But today, a touch of wheels, a tangle of legs and you'll be rich.

These are not cycling men. They are not Ambergs or Eglis, men soaked in the sweat of a decade's worth of cycling. These guys are capitalists, pure and simple. They sell tickets and it just so happens that cycling is in fashion, that we are in fashion, us funny foreigners with our exotic jerseys and strange accents, our glittering silver bikes and our ability to ride for days on end without rest. Their velodrome flits from town to town, taken apart and reassembled at lightning speed. It could be a circus for all they care, so long as it brings in the revenue.

I love the changing rooms and the camaraderie. The racers we'll never meet again, the friendships we'll store in our memory for who knows when. I love that American riders say "come to my house in Punxaphillyville" or wherever it is and they write down a house number and show photos of their girlfriend or mother, or both. There is a warmth and a sincerity you find almost nowhere else.

I take a fall in the third race. I'm proud to say I instigated it myself. My hand is out of joint, something about it looks unhand-like and it may be broken, or my wrist may be broken. I'm back on my bike though, and I've lost out on laps, someone got away before me. But I've earned my keep, and I won't have to work in a restaurant this time, we'll have plenty to get us through to the next race, and in between there will be food, cars, drink and girls – oh, the girls. I'll ride for the girls.

HELL
MONDAY 18TH JULY 1949

Hans Martin's sinuses were throbbing. Flashes of pain underlined his eyes and encircled his nose. The doctor looked down at him as he packed his instruments back into his oversized black bag. "You should go home, Hans Martin," he urged. "Go home, get some rest, and I do mean this – you could die."

Hans Man was a logical man who prepared for everything. Except his own death. Death had not been a scenario in his Tour de France roadmap. No thank you Doctor, death will not be an eventuality, absolutely not, we cannot have this Doctor, I must thank you, I really must but we have a Tour to win, there is no way we're not going to win this Tour and I will not be leaving my team here without my guidance. Now, if you please.

"Well, if you really must be so stubborn, Mr Martin, then we'll need to dose you up on penicillin, and please do avoid the high mountains. With your sinuses, things will only get worse."

Head pounding, Hans Martin scoured the perfumed streets of Grasse for a pharmacist, but not before leaving a very clear instruction for his team – do not attack early. Do not get involved in any breakaways, and above all, save your energy for the Izoard. I repeat, do not do anything stupid. Be circumspect and save your energy for a very long day in the saddle. We'll decide how to tackle Izoard after the Allos and the Vars.

The peloton left Grasse at the horrendously early hour of 5am in a heat that had brought out the undressed of Provence – crowds of people in pyjamas, ladies in bikinis and assorted states of half-nakedness. A number of riders took an especially long time to leave the town. Hans Martin, feeling dizzy and disoriented, tracked down his penicillin from an over-priced 24-hour pharmacy before bounding into the team car which sped in pursuit of the peloton.

"Some idiot's gone off the front," Bütschli the driver informed him. Hans Martin shook his head, took a swig of water to force down the penicillin, and grimaced. "I hope it's not one of ours. I've had enough headaches for one day already."

Bütschli pulled up alongside Jacques Goddet's car, allowing Hans Martin to lean out of the open window and request information. Even talking was painful.

"Hans Martin!" beamed Goddet. "So glad you're back in the land of the living."

Hans Martin flinched. "Yes. We'll see about that. Who's on the front?"

Goddet looked positively delighted. "Why, it's Ferdy Kübler!"

Retreating back into the vehicle, Hans Martin sank further into his seat. "Why do I even bother," he muttered to himself.

He ordered Buetschli to find Kübler, to get past the peloton and find the damn idiot. Buetschli swung round corners, overtaking riders and race motorcycles. Where the hell was Ferdy?

A full minute and a half ahead of the other riders, there he was, red jersey, white cross, arched back. Who else could it be?

"Fucking hell Ferdy, are you trying to kill me", screamed Hans Martin from the moving car, wincing at the effort. "Get back in the fucking peloton and save yourself. Jesus Christ."

Ferdy shrugged. Said he wanted to see how he felt, and he felt good. Hans Martin was not relieved.

Up to this point, the Tour had more or less gone to plan with only a Pyrenean hiccup. The Swiss had started the Tour with just six riders, with one place reserved for the mercurial Charly Guyot, the most talented rider of his or any generation, but Charly didn't respond to Hans Martin's calls and didn't turn up when requested.

Personnel issues aside, Hans Martin remained confident that his team could support Ferdy Kübler and make him the first Swiss rider ever to win a Grand Tour. The anti-clockwise loop through Brittany and down the west coast of France had brought the best out of his lead rider, including a time trial in which he finished 1'30" behind Fausto Coppi in second place, giving him second overall in the general standings. The Pyrenees would come ahead of the Alps and in hindsight, the 'Queen' day of the Tour was perhaps less traumatic than at first Hans Martin had experienced it. In one single stage, the riders ascended the Aubisque, the Tourmalet, the Aspin and Peyresourde, with Ferdy struggling to find his breath in the extreme heat and a series of punctures doing further damage to his already precarious mental state. Thinking on his feet, Hans Martin sent Georges Aeschlimann and Gopf Weilenmann back to pull Ferdy up the Tourmalet but above all, he gave them instructions to pull Ferdy's morale back up from the ravine down which it had fallen.

"You look great Ferdy," shouted Gopf. "Really good, just look at you!"

"The yellow jersey's blown", screamed Aeschlimann. "You can still do it Ferdy, you've still got it."

Aeschlimann wasn't wrong. Fiorenzo Magni, holder of the yellow jersey as leader of the general classification, would eventually blow on Peyresourde and the strategy of getting some positive thoughts into the head of Ferdy Kübler began to pay off as the Swiss pace quickened. Finishing 15 minutes behind Jean Robic and 11 behind Bartali – Hans Martin surmised that perhaps, after all, it wasn't such a bad day.

Yes, every moment of it felt like a living hell, but the end result was acceptable.

Hans Martin was, therefore, relieved to note that not only did Ferdy feel good, Ferdy had relented and had rejoined Robic, Coppi, Bartali and Lazaridès on the first climb of the day, the Allos. The weather had turned, too. The heat of Grasse had given way to cooler temperatures and heavy rain on the mountains. The penicillin was beginning to kick in and Hans Martin's mood was lifting. Ferdy had descended the Allos like a man possessed, resuming the upward gradient on the col de Vars alone with renewed vigour. He crested the Vars with nearly four minutes' lead over Robic, Coppi, Lazaridès and Stan Ockers, with Magni even further back.

At this point, Hans Martin realised, Ferdy Kübler was the virtual yellow jersey.

And then it all went wrong. Just after the rapid ascent of the Vars and its equally rapid descent, Ferdy's back wheel blew. Soaked, sodden and frozen, Ferdy simply couldn't work his pump. His fingers couldn't move, he couldn't grip anything. He sat by the side of the road, crying copiously. "I'll never win this Tour de France, never!" he yelled at Hans Martin who had found his rider in a most emotional state. Hans Martin repaired the puncture himself, gave Ferdy an almighty push and jumped back into the driver's seat himself, pushing Bütschli aside and promising Ferdy that he's still in yellow and he'll follow him down the mountain personally.

He turned the key and the car wheezed and spluttered. No, no, not now. He turned the key again, and all he could hear was the rain colliding with the windscreen. Hans Martin flew into a rage against the vehicle, pounding the steering wheel. Releasing the handbrake, he got out and started to push against the frame of the car, before jumping back in and guiding the car down the precarious slopes of the col de Vars, gently caressing the brake with his foot and hoping that gravity would do the rest. For the length of time that Hans Martin fought with the broken-down team car, he almost forgot the sinus pain. At each turn, he uttered a small prayer, please hold, please make sure the brakes hold, please don't let there be a break in the descent. At the bottom, when gravity had done its work and the car could move no further without propulsion, Hans Martin leapt from the vehicle and ran around the cafes and restaurants, asking for support. Barely anyone recognised him, until finally, in a bar down a backstreet, salvation - a Swiss fan offered him his Fiat and Hans Martin was able to rejoin the race.

How long had it been since he rescued Ferdy? Half an hour?

A second puncture had befallen poor Ferdy. Without a team car, Ferdy was alone and broken. Why will my pump not work? Why can't I get my pump to work? Tears streamed down his face, washed by the constant rain as he desperately sought anyone who could help. A new inner tube, that would save my race – somebody, help me! I need a pump and an inner tube. The Italian team car slowed down to catch a glimpse of the frenzied, anguished rider in the red jersey. Is that Kübler? *Che cosa succede?* Please give me an inner tube, please, somebody help me. They simply laughed and drove on, leaving Ferdy to his plight. A photographer had taken up position on the corner of the road. Why couldn't he help? Why did he have to just sit and take photographs?

Time passed. Bartali and Coppi also passed, without acknowledging him. An era seemed to pass. Robic, Lazarides, Ockers... Ferdy was no longer the yellow jersey on the road, he was no longer in contention and by the time Hans Martin did reach him in the borrowed Fiat, Ferdy was a broken man, staring disconsolately into the distance, rain – or tears – dripping from his face.

The pump worked perfectly well for Hans Martin.

Ferdy punctured again on the descent of Izoard, which he had ascended at walking pace, further compounding his dreadful day. Hans Martin once more had to leap from the car to repair Ferdy's wheel, and when Ferdy came in a full fifteen minutes behind Gino Bartali, there was little to be said.

Ferdy spent the night puking in his hotel bedroom, keeping his teammates awake with his wailing and his third-person shrieking. Hans Martin spent the night unable to sleep due to renewed sinus pain and the trauma of the day and he swore never, ever to come back to the Tour de France as long as he lived. Which, he reasoned, after a day like today might not be as long as he had hoped.

And yet the Tour carried on, as did Ferdy, as did Hans Martin. Through the snow of Iseran, they sought out soup and warmth while the race slipped ever further away from Ferdy and ever more towards the magnificent Fausto Coppi. Ferdy ploughed his lonely furrow, a sullen figure no longer sure of himself and no longer sure he even had a career.

On the rest day, as Ferdy and the Swiss team took to the roads to keep their legs in shape for the remainder of the Tour, a group of Swiss supporters noticed Ferdy, running alongside and screaming "Ferdy, Ferdy, we love you Ferdy", but Ferdy kept his head down, to the dismay of his teammates.

"A silent Ferdy is a dead Ferdy", remarked Gopf Weilenmann.

At the dinner table, Hans Martin presented his rider with steak.

"Not steak again", mumbled Ferdy, pushing it away.

Very well Ferdy, offered Hans Martin. You can have the fish instead. He presented him with a plate of fish.

"Not fish again".

Very well, Ferdy. You can have the soup instead.

"I'm sick of soup."

What Ferdy failed to notice that afternoon on the rest day was the reaction from the Swiss supporters. Whereas he had experienced the Tour as a succession of catastrophes, for the fans back home in Switzerland, Ferdy had become a national hero. Struck down multiple times by the famed Witch with Green Teeth, Ferdy had been the victim of ill fortune, yes, but most importantly, he had got back on his bike and he had tackled the most fearsome climbs of the Pyrenees and the Alps. While he may not be in yellow, he had found his way into Swiss hearts. Perhaps you don't have to win to be successful in life.

On reading of his elevation to *Ferdy Nationale* in the morning newspapers, he was persuaded to carry on despite his wretched health and his deteriorating mental state. After all, the next stage would finish over the border in Lausanne – a homecoming of sorts.

Ferdy wouldn't make it to Lausanne, however. Sick, tired and fed up, he was overtaken by Belgian sprinters on the San Bernardino climb, an insult so stinging that Ferdy climbed off his bike and got straight into the broom wagon which, he reasoned, was hovering suggestively.

Hearing that their hero had abandoned the race, the fickle Swiss cycling enthusiasts turned on their man. They collected up their 'Hop Ferdy' banners, threw them to one side and joined in a chorus of boos every time Ferdy's name was mentioned over the tannoy. The press equally turned. Jacques Goddet, organiser of the Tour, wrote in l'Equipe that while Ferdy may be an exceptional rider and an exceptional man, his abandonment on the San Bernardino climb was both sudden and inexplicable, even if he were as ill as he later claimed. How on earth could Ferdy Kübler not have found the extra resources from within to conquer the mountain and descend in glory to face his own adoring public? Were they not motivation enough? Perhaps this 'illness' of his stemmed from – and he shall not use these words lightly – "preparatory methods" employed by the

Swiss rider in order to recover from his endeavours in both the Pyrenees and the Alps?

In a word, doping. On reading these words, Ferdy's heart sinks. He has never taken so much as a vitamin pill in his entire career. He knows these pills circulate. He has seen riders inject themselves mid-race and throw the needle into hedgerows. He has seen things that would make riders' mothers weep, but out of respect for the sport and out of respect for his colleagues, he has said nothing. But to be accused... Ferdy viewed himself as a paragon of virtue. The word dropped on Ferdy like a bomb and would follow him for the remainder of the season.

As for Hans Martin and his remaining riders, the struggle continued on into Paris and around the customary revolutions of the Parc des Princes velodrome. Hans went straight home to Zürich after that, refusing to stay behind for the traditional post-Tour celebrations, refusing to talk to the press.

He wanted his bed. He wanted a holiday. He had had enough. He would see out his contract and return to managing trade teams, so long as he didn't have to manage Ferdy Kübler.

1950

GODS, ANGELS
AND HUGO
KOBLET

How do you win the Giro d'Italia? Until 1950, there had been one pre-requisite: you had to be Italian. Men like Girardengo, Binda and Guerra had written their names into legend, dominating what were quasi all-Italian affairs in the '20s and '30s before a young Gino Bartali took up the baton and more recently a young Fausto Coppi. More of than not, an Italian rider – whether he were a contender or not – would build his entire season around the Giro, more often than not foregoing the far less important Tour de France.

Nobody, not even Hugo Koblet, believed that Hugo Koblet would win the Giro in 1950. Had he ridden a Grand Tour before? No. Had he ridden for more than a week in the mountains before? No. Had any foreign rider ever won the Giro since its inception? No.

And yet there were signs, for those keen to read them.

In 1948, Hugo joined the Tebag team as *domestique* to Ferdy Kübler. That year, Ferdy won the Tour de Suisse and the newly created Tour de Romandie. Hugo's role was to work for Ferdy and given the opportunity once Ferdy had secured the position he wanted, to work for some stage wins in the final 50km. He was allowed to win the final stage of Romandie after having finished 2nd in the first stage between Geneva and Aigle. In the second stage of that Tour, Ferdy sent Hugo off up the road into Lugano with over a 3-minute advantage. With all eyes on Hugo, Ferdy rode more freely, but everyone kept their eyes on this *pistard* who suddenly crested mountains as if they were not there. Between Lugano and Arosa, Hugo fulfilled his duties of *domestique* by pulling Ferdy into the final stages of the final climb, finishing in an impressive 6th place.

But Hugo was not born into service, and Ferdy was not born to pay his bills on time. What should have been an easily resolvable dispute over bonus payments turned into a bickering feud overnight. Hugo didn't necessarily want the money – there would always be more money tomorrow – he just wanted to be recognised. If the two national Tours had taught him anything, it wasn't just that Ferdy needed him, it was that he could be the better rider.

Hugo quit the Tebag team and joined Cilo as team leader with the mercurial Charly Guyot in his service – whenever Charly Guyot decided he wanted to ride. Cilo won the team classification in Romandie, but just before the Tour de Suisse, Hugo was overturned by a car while out on a training ride near Bellinzona. His leg broke on impact, and his first season as team leader for Cilo was cut short.

So what does Hugo do when he can't ride? He falls in love with the daughter of a furniture shop owner. Fraulein Poehler was described by those who knew her as a headstrong beauty, others would call her a Teutonic Goddess. Teammates told reporters that of all the women Hugo Koblet would get involved with, and he would get involved with many, Poehler was the most magnificent, the most extraordinary of all, the only one who could truly be a match for Hugo.

And yet perhaps this would turn out to be their downfall. She opted to pursue her nursing studies in England for six months, leaving Hugo and his broken leg in Zürich. Hugo expected her to stay at his bedside, but he swallowed his pride and let her go. While Fraulein Poehler was away, Hugo discovered that he was not quite ready to devote himself entirely to just one woman. When she returned, ready to devote herself to a life of conjugal bliss, home-making and service to the handsome young cyclist, Hugo was back on two feet and back in the clubs and bars of Zürich with girls draped over his shoulders. With fresh eyes, she saw that her life of conjugal bliss would never materialise with this man, and she left him just before the 1950 Giro d'Italia, telling friends, reporters and magazines – indeed, anyone who would pay for an interview - that Hugo is not a "real man".

Not a real man. That could have stung. But Hugo's attitude to girls is revealed in a comment from his track partner of many years, Armin von Buren, who claimed that Hugo had once told him:

"I'm young, I'm carefree. I don't want to get married. You see that girl over there? She's honest, she's true. I'm not touching her because she'll think I'm in love with her and she'll break down when she discovers I'm not. But that girl over there? She's just after a good time. With that kind of girl, I have absolutely no scruples."

In the meantime, just before his rupture with Fraulein Poehler, Hugo gave everyone a glimpse of what might be in the Tour de Romandie of 1950. He attacked instantly in the first stage which would finish in Vevey and stuck to Ferdy Kübler throughout the race. In the penultimate stage to Vallorbe, he took the leader's green jersey with barely a bead of sweat on his forehead. The Swiss press remarked on the ease with which Hugo Koblet appeared to climb the harshest of gradients and how, after each stage, he would wash his face with a bottle of Perrier before speaking to them. A gentleman.

The final stage didn't go to plan, though. Hugo had selected the lightest available inner tubes without anticipating the gravel roads between Vallorbe and Geneva. A series of punctures cut his lead, giving the French rider Edouard Fachleitner the opportunity to push for victory. An opportunistic Ferdy Kübler also saw the chance for victory, latching on the Fachleitner's wheel and joining in furious relays with the Frenchman. Fachleitner dug deep and found some extra on the finish, winning the stage and ultimately winning the Tour by 51 seconds. Without the punctures, Hugo would have won Romandie by a sizeable margin, but without Ferdy Kübler pulling Fachleitner to the line, he may have won it regardless.

Until this moment, there had been a growing number of Koblet admirers who were equal admirers of Kübler. If the financial dispute of the previous year had gone largely unnoticed, this was the first noticeable split in the fan base. What it revealed, perhaps, was a friction in the country that few had bothered to notice until it had been exposed to them. For the young, urban, cosmopolitan city types, Hugo was a poster boy. Stylish, blonde, always well-turned out, Hugo was a breath of fresh air in a post-war peloton full of rugged old pre-war men like Bartali and Kübler. But if you were slightly older and of a more conservative leaning, and perhaps you clean your bins every Sunday, then what better rider could there be than Ferdy? The poor-man-come-good who fights for everything and stands for family values. He may not be pretty, but neither are we, and he's our man.

Kübleristes and Kobletistes had already started to pull in different directions.

Now, to put the disappointment of Romandie into context, Hugo had not seen this race as preparation for the Giro d'Italia. Indeed, he hadn't even considered riding the Giro at all. Teams had already been named, and Hugo didn't have a contract in Italy unlike Ferdy who would be riding for the Fréjus team alongside several other Swiss riders. No, Hugo's season had been cobbled together on the fly due to that broken leg the previous year. A couple of week-long stage races and perhaps the Swiss Nationals, little more than that.

One man had been watching Romandie closely, however. Learco Guerra, former Giro winner, former World Champion and now the owner of the Guerra outfit that would ride the Giro, had come to watch Attilio Magnaguagno, a Swiss-Italian rider. Attilio was badly out of sorts, coming in last of all. Koblet caught his attention though, and Guerra moved quickly to sign him up, shifting Magnaguagno unceremoniously out of the Giro team and Koblet straight into it alongside his good friends the Weilenmann brothers.

Guerra threw Hugo into Italian racing as a form of preparation, starting with a one-day race between Milan and Vicenza. It took Hugo some time to adapt to the Paris-Roubaix derailleurs that were fixed towards the back of the frame of the Guerra bicycles. Over the first 50km, Hugo lost 3 minutes on the peloton while fiddling with the contraption, but as he found his rhythm and got used to this new method of shifting gears, he went into pursuit mode. The flat roads of northern Italy smoothed out and Hugo reeled in the peloton, little by little. He didn't calculate, he employed no mathematics and no speed estimations, he simply rode to the maximum of his ability for as long as he could, catching the pack within the final 20km and staying within it until the finish.

This caught the attention of the race judges at the finish line who huddled together and awarded Hugo a penalty. The reason? For the 'unnatural manner in which Hugo Koblet – three minutes down on the peloton – managed to catch the other riders who were moving at high speed throughout.' In other words, it is not possible for a rider in 'natural circumstances' to achieve such a feat, therefore, we don't believe he's clean and we're penalising him, demoting him to last place.

Learco Guerra threw his arm around Hugo and smiled. You're so good, they think you're doping. And now you know how hard it is to win in Italy, young man. We're going to have a very interesting Giro d'Italia.

The Giro was billed very much as a battle between the three previous winners of the Tour de France. Jean Robic ('47), Gino Bartali ('48) and Fausto Coppi ('49), not forgetting the winner of the 1948 Giro, Fiorenzo Magni. Coppi had also won the Giro last year, completing the Grand Tour double and had started 1950 in sparkling form winning both Paris-Roubaix and the Flèche-Wallonne, a new race held in French-speaking Belgium.

Unlike the Tour, the Giro was made up of trade teams, and for the first time, some of those trade teams were led by foreigners. Ferdy Kübler was designated team leader for Fréjus-Superga, while fellow Swiss rider Fritz Schär was named leader of Arbos. Another first for this year's Giro – the Tour would start, rather than end, in Milan. The finish line would, for the first time, be in Rome to mark the Pope's jubilee year – and the peloton would be invited to meet the pontiff after the final stage. Cycling is, after all, an acceptable alternative to Catholicism.

Swiss journalists had mostly stayed at home. After all, the Giro is a race for Italians. It's hard to keep peoples' attention for three weeks on what is essentially a national championships that happens to include a few foreigners. They hadn't reckoned on one of their own claiming the *maglia rosa* as soon as the second day on the stage between Salsomaggiore and Firenze. A train heaving with hastily packed suitcases and underprepared journalists entered town late that night.

Schär's lead was a surprise, and even more surprisingly, it lasted throughout the mostly flat first week as the riders wended their way without much event towards the Dolomites and the north-east of the country where, after a rest day, the main action of the Giro would start. It was a *drôle de guerre*, Fritz Schär growing into his pink jersey as each day ticked down, a huddle of Swiss journalists hanging on his every post-stage word. Italian journalists respected the jersey, making time for the man who earned their respect two years previously by finishing 3rd in Lombardia. Hugo Koblet won the final stage before the rest day but once more, his chances were dismissed for the usual reasons – first Grand Tour, here to win a couple of stages, will probably go home before the next rest day...

After that first rest day in Locarno, Fritz Schär lost time on the day's winner Maggini and eventually lost the pink jersey. The Swiss journalists, believing the game to be up, starting packing their bags. We've had a good run, our boys have done well but the Giro reverts to type now. The Italians are back. What a shame, then, for those who did catch the first train to have missed the stage from Brescia to Vicenza.

The riders had mostly dozed through the first 100km until Pasquale Fornara and Hugo Koblet attacked with around 75km to go. Together, they climbed the Passo Xon and then the Fugazze. Koblet gained in strength to lead over the second and take the extra minute's bonus that was available. Behind, chaos ensued as riders realised the gap wasn't being brought down. Magni fell, so did Coppi while attempting to avoid a rider slipping in front of him. He rode on, 5th on the day but 3 minutes behind Hugo.

Now wearing the *maglia rosa*, was Hugo here to stay? Pasquale Fornara, for one, was impressed. "Hugo is a champion. He's incredibly strong," was all he had to say at the finish line, puffing out his cheeks in admiration.

The next stage from Vicenza to Bolzano would take in over 270km, over the Rolle, the Pordoi and the Gardena. An early crash, perhaps caused by jitters in the peloton, saw Fausto Coppi fall heavily. Word got through from rider to rider that Fausto wasn't moving. They'd seen him fall, they'd heard a sound like bone snapping. Chinese whispers moved through the peloton; some thought their chance had come. A Giro *senza Fausto*. Robic let fly over the Rolle, pursued by Koblet and the minuscule Italian climber Astrua. Robic took the minute's bonus at the top and they were joined on the descent by Bartali, the old man sensing an opportunity with Fausto on his way to hospital.

Well, one shouldn't dwell.

Robic and Bartali pounced when Hugo punctured. "He's blown", yelled Bartali, and both men rose out of their saddles and stomped on the pedals. It's Romandie all over again thought Hugo, standing distraught by the roadside. He saw them disappear around a bend and got to work on his puncture in the absence of a team car.

And then, in an echo of that one-day race from Milan to Vicenza, Hugo went into pursuit mode. Italian journalists wrote in awe of this beautiful track-rider's posture, his time-triallist demeanour. He reached the Pordoi to find Robic and Bartali open-mouthed. What the hell do we have to do to get rid of you? Hugo distanced Bartali over the Pordoi and soon they were joined by Ferdy Kübler who had at one stage been over four minutes behind the leading group but had descended like a demon, risking life and limb down the hairpins. Did Ferdy allow Hugo to draft him, as if they were teammates once more? Robic and Bartali swapped glances with the Swiss riders – how dare they allow nationhood to influence the Giro d'Italia! A final puncture, this time by Robic, meant that three men would ride into Vicenza, Gino Bartali taking the win with Koblet and Kübler just behind.

With Bartali 5 minutes behind in the general classification, Italians began to take Hugo Koblet seriously. Perhaps he has filled out. Perhaps he is more mature. Perhaps he can last the full three weeks. Perhaps he should be stopped.

Learco Guerra knew more than anyone that Hugo was in danger. What, for example, was Bartali's *soigneur* doing in the kitchen that evening when Bartali's team were staying in a different hotel? Night after night, Learco Guerra lived on edge, watching slippery *soigneurs* and shady masseurs slithering down darkened corridors. "A mafia of sorts is acting against my young rider," he told journalists.

Hugo was booked into rooms in which he would never step. Guerra would swap Hugo's room with that of another rider, only to discover that the other rider would develop stomach cramps and would spend the night vomiting. Not once did Hugo receive a meal that was intended for him from a hotel kitchen. Learco Guerra took care of everything himself, wrapping Hugo in cotton wool.

Day after day the attacks came, mostly from Bartali attempting to cut into Hugo's lead. They exchanged bonus minutes as the Tour approached its penultimate stage between Campobasso and Naples. Only mechanical issues could realistically prevent Hugo from winning the Giro; those hopes were raised when he punctured four times, each time when alone. Ferdy Kübler also punctured four times, and Gino Bartali had escaped with a significant margin.

Hugo and Ferdy found themselves together, alone. They rode furiously, putting their newfound rivalry behind them, providing a remarkable contrast. Ferdy's erratic movements, his arched back, Hugo's perfect posture and apparent stillness. Each man taking equal turns, they cut into Bartali's lead, each gradient an opportunity to power harder through the cranks, to find extra seconds that Bartali may not have found, each corner cut giving a few extra inches. The final heroic act of this 1950 Giro would not belong to Gino Bartali, it would belong to Hugo Koblet and Ferdy Kübler.

Was Hugo's victory marred by the absence of Fausto Coppi as some devilishly suggested in the press? Far from it. Coppi had struggled to maintain the pace in the first week, losing over three minutes to Hugo. Opposing voices in the media reminded the nay-sayers that Hugo not only had to see off Gino Bartali but Kübler, Magni, Bresci, Lazarides, Robic, Maggini and a mafia of soigneurs looking to poison his evening meals. Most would rightly recognise Koblet's victory in the 1950 Giro d'Italia as 'imperious', 'majestic' and 'unbeatable', and any doubts simply vanished when Hugo stood before the Pope speaking perfect Italian at a reception held on the Monday after the final stage in Rome.

Well – he may not be Italian. He may not even

be Catholic, but he rides with such grace and such speed that he may as well be one of ours. The first foreign winner of the Giro d'Italia had been claimed by the Italians, as he would be claimed everywhere he rode. With a comb in his back pocket and a bottle of cologne for special occasions, Hugo Koblet had the girls flocking behind him wherever he went. He was the young superstar the sport had been unknowingly craving – a bridge to the younger generations, a filmstar on two wheels, and a true gentleman. An envious Ginaccio watched on as Hugo was welcomed by the pontiff and then met a young Swiss-Italian girl later that day, taking her in his arms and kissing her in front of a spellbound audience.

"Hugo Koblet kissed me! I'll never wash again," she told her friends.

I HATE HUGO KOBLET

In the early summer of 1950, a journalist following the Criterium du Dauphiné Libéré, a week-long stage race which overlaps with the Tour de Suisse, was enjoying a glass of chilled Macon on the terrasse at a restaurant in Annecy. He was admiring the view of the lake, waxing lyrical about the Venetian aspect of this beautiful town, preparing his notes for the following day. A sparkling summer, he noted, only adds to the beauty of this *ville Savoyarde*.

The Dauphiné wasn't providing him with an awful lot to write about.

A familiar voice then called out from the table behind him. *"Garçon! Deux bières, s'il vous plaît."*

The journalist looked around to see the square jaw and frizzy mop of André Mahé, a Breton rider who – curiously – was meant to be riding in the Tour de Suisse, not the Dauphiné. Indeed, André Mahé was supposed to be riding in tomorrow's stage which would see the riders complete their loop around German and Italian-speaking Switzerland, back into Zürich.

"André, dear boy, what on earth are you doing here?"

André Mahé's eyes sparkled and his whole face transformed into a welcome smile.

"I quit the race," he replied, joining the journalist at his table. "What's the point when you're riding against Hugo Koblet?"

The Breton went on to explain that he believed himself to be a capable rider, if not better than that on a good day. Someone who could compete at the highest level. And yet, while climbing the Lukmanier, he found himself lashing the pedals with every last ounce of energy he had remaining, sweat pouring from his brow. He was suffering, in short. He looked across to his right, where he found he was being overtaken by a quite serene Hugo Koblet, one hand on his handlebar, the other holding his lunch.

"And do you know what he did next? He pulled a comb out of his pocket and started grooming himself. I don't mind being outclassed, but I don't like people taking the piss out of me."

Hugo gave a gentlemanly wave and accelerated past Mahé with such ease that the Frenchman decided on the spot to quit the race.

I hate Hugo Koblet, he laughed. He's got it all.

Hugo had returned from the Giro to the acclamation of all Switzerland. A few months ago, hardly anyone had heard of Hugo Koblet, and now the world and its mother was discussing *le bel Hugo* and all of

Zürich has turned out to see the blonde angel who conquered Gino Bartali, the man who became the first foreign winner of the Giro d'Italia, oh – and the first Swiss rider ever to win a Grand Tour. Hugo's image adorns all the front pages, the name Koblet screams from the newsstands. He is given a hero's homecoming, and it could hardly go unnoticed that the proportion of young women lining the streets had grown significantly, too.

Since they had last seen him – if they had noticed at all – Hugo Koblet had undergone something of a transition. Winning a Grand Tour can change a man. It is as if Hugo has grown in stature – literally. As if he has grown several inches. He sports sunglasses in the style of an American film star, every move is scrutinised and commented upon, from the comb in the back pocket to the bottle of Perrier at the end of each stage which he uses to wash his face before meeting journalists and photographers.

The Tour de Suisse of 1950 was squeezed in between the two Tours of Italy and France, offering the public the opportunity to see their new idol alongside that other rider whose name begins with K, what's his name again... oh yes, Ferdy Kübler. Poor Ferdy had believed that he alone represented Switzerland on the international stage. Hugo's rise may not have been a surprise in cycling terms, but the reverence for *le bel Hugo* rankled with Ferdy. It was, remember, Ferdy Kübler who had worn yellow in the Tour de France, it was Ferdy who held Fausto to a draw at the Oerlikon as a youngster, it was Ferdy who had won this race many times over. He seethed inside, watching his popularity ebb away, towards someone younger and prettier than him.

The peloton left Zürich, as was tradition, and headed for Winterthur where the Luxembourg rider Jan Goldschmidt took the stage victory and with it the yellow jersey. In Liesthal the next day, he consolidated his place as leader but Hugo's time trialling cut the lead significantly the day after that. Ferdy lost over a minute to Hugo on the time trial, shedding on average a second for every kilometre.

The next morning was the first true test of the Tour, a climb of the Oberalp. The two K's led from the front with eyes only for each other. Each furious Kübler attack was repelled with insulting ease by Koblet while Louison Bobet – who was beginning to regret having chosen the Tour de Suisse over the Dauphiné – struggled to keep up with the Swiss duo. Ferdy's luck ran out on the descent with first a puncture and then a fall on the Lukmanier on which André Mahé had been so comprehensively humiliated. With Hugo Koblet pedalling off into the valley, Ferdy lay among the stones and the dirt and thought seriously about joining Mahé and catching the train to Annecy for a chilled glass of Macon. Ferdy finished over 20 minutes back on Hugo that day and spent the evening fulminating in his hotel bedroom.

On the penultimate stage into St. Moritz, Ferdy attacked on Hugo's first puncture and his team director quickly realised that if Hugo were to puncture again, Ferdy might have the opportunity to claw back a large amount of time on his rival. Jan Goldschmidt, former yellow jersey, provided the foil for Ferdy, a slipstream into which he could ride. The news reached Ferdy that Hugo had indeed punctured again, and again, and again. Four punctures to Ferdy's two, and the gap kept on climbing. Behind, Hugo alternated between repairing and time-trialling, conceding that he may puncture at any moment, so in between, race to the limit and consider a puncture an opportunity to breathe. In time, the punctures got further apart, the time-trialling got smoother.

Seeing Hugo appear in the distance and steadily pull himself to the front of the race was enough for Ferdy to abandon hope, to power himself down and concede the race. There's nothing I can do, he reasoned. In a straight-up race between myself and Hugo Koblet, I lose. They crossed the line together, smiles for photographers. They even shared the bouquets of flowers and rode side-by-side for the crowds.

This is the new normal, thought Ferdy. This is how it's going to be.

ALEX BURTIN'S SUMMER HOLIDAY

Alex Burtin had planned a summer trip with his family, walking in the valleys not far from his home in Lausanne. In January, he had rolled out maps on the dining room floor, plotted routes, made notes and planned stopovers. Itineraries were created, restaurants were chosen and – Alex Burtin's family would whisper to each other – the schedule would appear to be much the same as last year and the year before that, and the year before that too.

Life is simple, thinks Alex Burtin. If you make it so.

Alex Burtin is a man for whom bullet points may have been invented. Stoic in manner and appearance, age has rounded him, smoothed the sharpened contours of the amateur cyclist he used to be. He prefers slightly creased white shirts, slightly creased grey trousers. Nothing too complicated, nothing that would impinge upon more vital decisions.

When Hans Martin handed in his resignation as Technical Director of the Swiss National Team after the diabolical World Championships of 1949, Alex Burtin structured his thoughts in what might be described henceforth as a Burtinesque fashion:

- I read the news that Hans Martin had resigned
- I reflected upon the situation at hand
- I decided to apply for the role
- I prepared for the interview
- I am now Technical Director of the Swiss National Team

Alex Burtin simply moved his walking holiday to the end of August and started making plans for the Tour de France. And when Alex Burtin reads in the national press that he is not, perhaps, the number one choice of most columnists and indeed far from the number one choice of his star rider Ferdy Kübler, he reflects upon his decision further and resolves to work harder. After all, there are many things that Alex Burtin cannot influence. Hans Martin is a younger man than he, and therefore held stronger personal relationships with the riders. Alex Burtin is the wrong side of 50 and his years in cycling are long forgotten by both public and the current crop of young riders. We are not alike, he muses, and therefore we cannot approach the role the same way.

And so, as it becomes clear that Hugo Koblet will bypass the Tour de France after his Giro d'Italia win, Alex Burtin is left with a team that fundamentally revolves around the doubting Ferdy Kübler and a talented group of riders whose motivation is to be the second-best Swiss rider behind Ferdy. From what he understands, they would rather be second in the Swiss team and 69th overall than 3rd in the Swiss team and 25th overall.

This is a problem, Alex Burtin notes. A problem for which there must be a simple solution. His first decision is to create a *caisse commune*, a shared pot into which all winnings are returned and shared out equally between all riders. What better way to create solidarity and a common focus than by sharing the money equally between us? We have one man to fight for, he reasons. Therefore, if we fight equally, we win equally. Life is simple, why make matters more complicated by fighting?

Alex Burtin then makes the decision to arrive in France a full week ahead of his team in order to better familiarise himself with the surroundings, the organisers and the organisation of the race itself. The organisers themselves are delighted to have a *Romande* representing their Swiss cousins. How thoughtful. They welcome Alex Burtin with open arms, allowing him space within their offices to sit and read the race book at his leisure, allowing him to join them for evening drinks and pepper them with questions about regulations and suchlike. Messrs Goddet and Lévitan indulge their Francophone friend over *steak frites* and Chinon, along the way passing down anecdotes of Tours gone by.

And so, to the arrival of the riders. It would be a nice touch, Alex Burtin reflected, if he were there to welcome them personally at the Gare de l'Est station in Paris with a minibus. Take their bags. The personal touch. He would drive the bus himself, take them to the hotel, show them to their rooms. Hans Martin would never have done this. A new regime is in charge now. He would ask the riders to relax, take some time after a long journey and later they would dine at the hotel restaurant where, after pudding, he would reveal his plan for the *caisse commune* and how all would fight for Ferdy Kübler and the yellow jersey.

Alex Burtin had not reckoned on his riders' reticence to contribute to a shared pot. Bike racers, they are a strange breed.

He was to learn, and learn quickly, that building a team around Ferdy Kübler would require more than the promise of shared earnings. There were some riders who would die for Ferdy. Emilio Croci-Torti, for one, would lay prostrate at the wheels of a furious peloton for his friend. On the other hand, there was Gottfried Weilenmann who was one of a growing number of riders who would call themselves 'Kobletistes'. Not exactly anti-Kübler, at least not yet, but a dedicated friend of Hugo Koblet and – more than that – a capable rider in his own right. He had won last year's Tour de Suisse, defeating his Tour de France teammate Georges Aeschlimann, and the very idea of playing *gregario* to that never-do-well Ferdinand Kübler rankled. He grumbles to his friends – I climbed the Gotthard. I defeated the Furka. I rode into Davos alone, and I can damn well win this Tour de France.

Alex Burtin, seeing things simply, rejected this world view. Weilenmann was not a Grand Tour winner.

If this Swiss team were modest and fractured, the Italians could be described as fearsome yet depleted. Last year's Tour winner Fausto Coppi does not start due to what could be a career-ending injury suffered in the Giro d'Italia. We may never see him ride again. There is Gino Bartali, the pious old man of pre-war Tours and champion of 1948. Fiorenzo Magni too, the eternal third man who could win this race were he not in the same team as Bartali.

And then there's the French. They have Géminiani and the young prince Bobet. There's no room for the winner of three years ago, Jean Robic. He has to ride for the Breton team while Belgium have brought Stan Ockers, surely a future Tour winner, capable in all spheres.

The only way Ferdy Kübler can win this Tour, Alex Burtin realises, is for the entire team to work for him.

Ferdy may have doubted Alex Burtin's capabilities, but he came to this Tour with several suitcases full of self-doubt. He doubted he could ever win a Grand Tour, he doubted that his body or his bicycle could stretch to three gruelling weeks of bike racing. Last year was still fresh in the memory, and so was the embarrassment of 1947.

You could also argue that Koblet's ascendancy had left a mark on Ferdy, too. Few had noticed that he finished fourth in the Giro d'Italia, and few even noticed how he pulled Hugo to the front of the race in the penultimate stage, effectively saving his pink jersey. So many times during that Giro, he had gone into the red and each time, nobody noticed. They were all looking at handsome Hugo, all too busy falling in love with him while Ferdy did all the work. Ferdy didn't have to help that day. He didn't have to ride so hard. Sometimes he regrets it.

The Tour de France, riders, *caravane* and all, left Paris for Metz on the morning of the 13th July. It would be a stage that heralded a return to the old, heroic days of bike racing with 307km of utter boredom, the first of three stages longer than 300km over the next three weeks. Modern racing is about shorter stages, they complained, more about athleticism and strength than endurance and good fortune. Nothing happened. The only excitement came at the start of the stage when Orson Welles sent the riders off, a star-struck Ferdy telling everyone who would listen that he had shaken Orson's hand and that he might never wash again.

In the second stage from Metz to Lille, Gottfried Weilenmann's resistance broke at the same moment as his wheel fell apart on the pot-holed roads of Belgium. The Kobletiste would have to turn Kübleriste if he were to make anything of this summer and the idea of the *caisse commune* gathered momentum as one more rider belatedly warmed to Alex Burtin's idea.

The first week was a *drôle de guerre*, a phony war with the main protagonists keen not to show their hand too soon. Magni had worn yellow, Ockers had won a stage, but the other contenders kept themselves anonymous within the peloton, saving energy for later stages. The French press led an ill-advised invective against the Italian team whose strategy, they wrote, was 1) to suck wheels, 2) to win the final sprint and 3) to smile innocently for the photographers. The French team, on the other hand, was valiantly trying to bring this Tour to some semblance of life; they deserve all of the 'kisses from the girls' at the finish line, not like those sneaky Italians who are ruining the sport of cycling for everyone, how dare they.

Not one writer suspected how much their words would come to haunt them.

The 6th stage was a Breton time trial – from Dinard to Saint-Brieuc. It was also Ferdy Kübler's first opportunity to show his hand, an opportunity to break the rules.

Alex Burtin first realised that Ferdy Kübler was going to wear a silk jersey the morning of the time trial out of Dinard. He remonstrated with his rider. Alex Burtin had, after all, consumed the Tour regulations and was able to regurgitate them word-by-word. I didn't read that book for my enjoyment, Mr Kübler, he would point out in his customary matter-of-fact fashion. I read that book to protect my riders. It states, very clearly, that you are not allowed to wear a silk jersey.

Ah, but I can and I shall, replied his rider. Ferdy wears silk for the time trial and Ferdy will win the time trial, and if Ferdy takes a penalty then it will be worth it because Ferdy will have won by over a minute.

Alex Burtin withdraws from the fight. You cannot win arguments with people who refer to themselves in the third person, he reflects.

Ferdy's gamble paid off. He overtook Géminiani, who had left 6 minutes before him and took the stage win with a 17-second advantage over Fiorenzo Magni. His silk jersey earned him a 15-second penalty, a penalty that Alex Burtin could not contest as it still meant that Ferdy had won the stage, and rules were rules. Ferdy was now 4 minutes and 35 seconds ahead of Gino Bartali and just 49 seconds behind his good friend Jean Goldschmidt, who was keeping the yellow jersey warm.

Meanwhile, the French media pressed on with their campaign against the Italians. Those listening to Georges Briquet on French radio would have heard him rail continually against the "green curtain" that had fallen across the Tour de France. An Italian team that had killed off all competition by controlling the race through their B-team which was working for Bartali and Magni while stealing stages after everyone else – notably the French team – had done all the hard work. Strong words, and words that were reflected in the general ambiance as the peloton arrived at the velodrome in Bordeaux where three Italians found themselves mixed up with two Frenchmen – Géminiani and Desbats – as well as one Belgian in Briek Schotte. The sound of whistling was deafening as the crowd vented their anger at the

Italian team, an anger that carried through to the peloton the next day when Belgian rider Maurice Blomme struck Magni with a clean left hook. Take that.

A second rest day in Pau was an opportunity to calm the nerves. Ferdy stayed in his hotel where Yvette Horner came to serenade him and his teammates with her accordion, along with some local boy scouts. Yvette and her boy scouts went door to door, dragging photographers along with them. In the meantime, Bartali and Magni went to Lourdes for Pious Gino to pray and for Magni to wait until Pious Gino had stopped praying. It would be a long time. While Gino was praying, Jean Robic was telling the rapturous French media that he would go on the attack against the Italian team in the Pyrenees, seeking revenge against Bartali for his attack in the Dolomites.

True to his word, then, Robic did attack on the first climb of the stage the next day on the Aubisque while Ferdy remained two minutes behind alongside Louison Bobet, Ockers and Meunier. Bartali could be found a further minute back, as was his habit after a rest day. Come the Tourmalet though, Bartali had found his legs, and Ferdy had lost his.

Something had woken Gino up from his post-rest-day slumber. Climbing the Tourmalet alongside Bresci, Sabatini and Leoni, Emilio Croci-Torti, the Italian-speaking Swiss rider and good friend of Ferdy, had to use his pump to stop French fans from attacking the Italian riders among screams of "macaroni" and other such pasta-related insults. The ill-feeling that had been stirred up by the French journalists was beginning to boil over in the heat and the drunkenness of the Pyrenean mountains. Bartali accelerated to join the group with Bobet, Robic and Ockers, reaching the top of the Aspin in a battle with Louison Bobet to take the 20-second bonus at the summit.

It was shortly afterwards that Bartali and Robic both collided with a photographer. Both men down, those crowds that had been whipped up by anti-Italian sentiment and no shortage of alcohol, descended on Bartali – or so Bartali thought. A man with a knife bore down upon him as he lay on the ground, although some would later say that it was a butter knife and he meant well. The butter knife was for baguette, not Bartali. But in the heat of the midday sun and the heat of the action, who can tell good intentions from bad? A petrified Bartali jumped back on his machine and escaped while behind, Magni rode through spit and insults.

Ferdy descended the Tourmalet at high speed, eventually succumbing to a broken wheel which saw him fall behind the front group. Gino Bartali won the sprint and Fiorenzo Magni took back the yellow jersey. Gino could have carried on riding all the way back to Italy, but instead he threw his bike to one side and stormed off.

Ferdy, despite his bad luck, now found himself second behind Magni in the general classification and considered it not such a bad day after all.

And then two things happened.

Ferdy accepted a ride back to his hotel from a man who would later be described in the newspapers as 'some bloke'. A member of the public, a nobody. Just someone with a car. The 'bloke' may have been trying to impress Ferdy. After all, it's not often you have a Tour de France legend in your front passenger seat, so he drove fast, perhaps smiling, perhaps telling Ferdy about his car and how fast it can go. Except that driving fast on wet roads is as ill-advised as cycling fast on wet roads, and the car left the road. The driver lost control of the vehicle which flipped over twice, landing against a building. Among the broken glass and the crumpled metal was the man who currently lay second in the Tour. Horrified residents came out to witness the scene. Chinese whispers spread like wildfire until they reached journalist Walter Grimm who learned that Ferdy Kübler was in hospital, out of the Tour de France and potentially dead. Who knows.

Instead, Ferdy was fine. A little shaken, but uninjured and – for once in his Grand Tour career – fortunate. The first Alex Burtin heard of the incident was when his rider walked in through the doors of the hotel and announced that he had been involved in a 'minor accident'. Alex Burtin reprimanded himself for not driving Ferdy Kübler to the hotel himself, and made a mental note never, ever again to leave him unattended.

At the same moment as Walter Grimm arrived at the Swiss team hotel, those rumours about Ferdy were dying down only to be replaced by another, more scandalous rumour. The Italians were leaving the race.

Grimm was dumbstruck. How could they leave the race? They had just won the stage in St. Gaudens and they have the yellow jersey. Grimm doubled back, racing across town to the Italian team hotel where he found doors closed and men in impeccable suits pacing up and down hotel corridors, gesticulating wildly at each other while chain-smoking cigarettes. Behind one door, Jacques Goddet was attempting to force Gino Bartali into a u-turn. I'm not putting my family through this one more day, fumed the latter. In another room, Fiorenzo Magni was admiring his yellow jersey and hoping to carry on riding while in another room, the B-team were quietly hoping and praying that Goddet could work his magic and convince Bartali to carry on the race.

Goddet continued for several hours in vain. Bartali could not be persuaded and along with team director Alfredo Binda, they pulled both the A and the B team out of the Tour, including yellow jersey wearer Magni who would grumble later that Bartali was looking for a way out of a Tour that he knew he could never win again at the age of 36.

The next morning, Ferdy Kübler was given the yellow jersey just 30 minutes before the start but he refused to wear it saying that he wanted to earn it on the road.

Now, there are voices who suggest that the departure of the Italian teams is a stroke of good fortune for Ferdy Kübler. Remove Magni and Bartali from the equation and the Tour is ultimately winnable. Neither Ferdy nor Alex Burtin went along with this opinion. As leader, you are a target. Better to pass unnoticed – as had been the plan – take time out of other riders in time trials and stick to the wheels in the mountains while waiting for a chance, should the chance come. Most people believed that Ferdy would blow at some point – he always does. Now Ferdy would have to ride against Ockers, Géminiani and Bobet, all of whom believed that the Tour was wide open.

The stage from Perpignan to Nimes took place on the hottest day of the year so far. Two north-African riders in Marcel Molines and Abdelkader Zaaf had broken away, and nobody in the peloton particularly wanted to chase them down. Indeed, everyone was quite happy for them to have the day to themselves. Ferdy twice suffered punctures and had to chase back to the group. His team dropped back to help, but not one of them could hang on to his wheel. At the same time, Abdelkader Zaaf was gasping and asking for water by the roadside. Instead, he was given two bottles of wine and would finish his Tour underneath a tree, drunk for the first – and final – time in his life.

With Ferdy back at the front of the peloton, a shout went up that Géminiani had broken a wheel. Stan Ockers leapt out in front in search of time on his rivals. Ferdy followed while Bobet languished behind, unable to react. The Frenchmen came in 10 minutes behind their rivals, their Tours effectively over. They may as well have been drinking wine under a tree with Zaaf.

Alex Burtin knew that with the Alps behind them, Louison Bobet could still claw back that time and was therefore still a rival. Stan Ockers had a formidable team around him, too. There was no such thing as guaranteed victory and Ferdy felt the same way. He was one of only two men the next day to refuse the opportunity to jump into the sea in Saint-Maxime as the thermometer hit 40 degrees in the shade. There's no need to waste time splashing about in the Mediterranean when there are fans with hoses by the roadside ready to cool you down.

Alex Burtin knew that the Alps held fresh memories of pain and suffering for Ferdy. Izoard in particular. He did all he could to distract Ferdy from the prospect of the fearsome Izoard, to boost his morale and convince him that he could finish the task at hand, that he – like Hugo before him – could win a Grand Tour. He would read him excerpts from the French press whose demolition job of the Italian team had concluded, their attention now on the yellow jersey.

Ferdy, listen to this. "In this peloton, Ferdy Kübler is a role model. His rivals all admire the careful and methodical approach he has taken to this Tour. He sees everything, he knows everything."

Ferdy sat up. This was not the Ferdy everyone had been expecting. In previous years, Ferdy would be dropping back to rival team cars, leaning into the window of various Technical Directors, saying "Ferdy goes on the attack now, are you ready?" and prodding his rivals every now and then with "Ferdy's going – anyone coming?" A Ferdy attack would be telegraphed in advance, often for fun, often contrary to the advice of his team manager whoever that may have been at the time. Ferdy wore managers down, blatantly ignoring and flouting instruction, taking part in insane breakaways that would break him. This year? No such thing.

But he still felt echoes of '49 as the clouds gathered on the col de Vars and the Izoard. The wind had whipped up, the temperatures had dropped. Looking ahead at the sparce mountain tops, the nerves returned. Bobet would attack. Ockers would chip away at his lead. There's still time for everything to fall apart.

Bobet did get away early, and Ferdy did puncture early. Ockers pulled from the front, using his strong Belgian team to full effect. Robic took turns, too, while Bobet developed a full minute's lead with Izoard still to come. Puncture repaired, Ferdy leapt back on his bike and rode so hard that he would reach the peloton ahead of the climb to the obvious surprise of Jean Robic who patted him on the back and whistled admiringly.

At the front, Bobet continued to stretch away up Izoard, writing his own legend as he rode while Ferdy, 3 minutes back, quietly wrote his. Instead of attacking to cut the gap down, he managed it while at the same time keeping Ockers firmly behind his wheel. This year, Ferdy would defeat Izoard, defeat his own demons and ride down into Briançon to take second place on the stage ahead of Ockers, taking the bonus seconds for himself and keeping nearly a 3-minute lead into the final mountain stage of the race. Journalists approached to shake him by the hand, congratulating him for winning the Tour, for the calmness and the strength with which he controlled the chase.

If the media had called it already, the French team had not. Alex Burtin had developed a sort of camaraderie with Jean Bidot, the Burtinesque French Technical Director, who had suggested – over a bottle of the red stuff – that Bobet still had it in him to retrieve that deficit. They laughed, but Alex Burtin took it seriously.

Bidot had a plan. The stage from Briançon to Saint-Etienne was a long one, 291km to be exact. The plan revealed itself at the first feeding station at the Pont de Laix, shortly after the Lautaret climb had been packed away for another year. Géminiani and Bobet attacked, carving out a two-minute lead over Ferdy. Bobet went alone as Géminiani faded and was caught by the group that included Kübler. Gem's job was to put the brakes on the Kübler group, staying at the front and slowing it down as much and as often as he could. Bobet's furious pace meant that the race was 40 minutes ahead of schedule.

As the day developed however, Bobet's will sapped. His reserves were depleting and 57km from the finish line, the Kübler group could see Bobet in the distance. However, as he felt the ground raise beneath his pedals on the col de la Republique, Louison found even greater reserves, bouncing from hairpin to hairpin. Those reserves would fizzle out towards the top as he learned – to his cost - that they are to be managed, not wasted, and he would soon be integrated into the chase group which would become the main group, which would eventually spit him out of the back and leave him behind. Louison can't go on.

The Tour was Ferdy's, and perhaps he knew it when he turned to Géminiani and said "Gem, you're fresh, you can win this. Go for it."

Géminiani took that stage 30 seconds ahead of Ferdy and over 6 minutes ahead of Louison Bobet whose time would come, just not this year. For Ferdy, all that remained was a 98km time trial from Saint Etienne to Lyon.

Alex Burtin prepared Ferdy's meal for him three hours before he was due to start. A simple bowl of soup, a veal escalope and some rice. They planned his warm-up, a 17-km ride which would take in a 700m climb, the first 17km of the time-trial route in fact. Ferdy took one look at his chainring and shook his head, I can't ride with that – change it Alex. So Alex Burtin changed it. Ferdy rode a quick circle before jumping off. I can't ride with that – change it Alex. So Alex Burtin changed it again. And again. And again, until Ferdy was finally satisfied with his setup.

The time trial, as expected, was a triumph. Ferdy swallowed up Louison Bobet after just 25km and finished over 5 minutes ahead of Stan Ockers in a performance that reminded many journalists present that day of Fausto Coppi's ride from Nancy to Colmar in the '49 Tour, a ride where Coppi ground his opponents into the tarmac with a gentlemanly disdain. You would be hard-pushed to find anyone who disagreed. The writer Albert Baker d'Isy reminded everyone that Kübler had come to this Tour with a team of just six riders while Belgium and Italy came with teams of ten – twenty if you count the Italian B-team. Indeed, he was on his own in the mountains, his team only able to support on the easier flat stages.

Ferdy and the rest of the peloton took a ceremonial ride into Paris with streets lined with hundreds of thousands of fans and well-wishers. There was nothing to worry about that day, no attacks would come, the temperature temperate, the roads smooth, the task simple. Ferdy had won the Tour de France sooner than he had realised and although he sometimes wondered whether he would have done so had the Italians remained in the competition, he thought back to Izoard and the time trials, to the times he could have cracked – and would have cracked in previous years – and thought how much easier it actually was this time around. How much simpler it was.

How much simpler everything is when Alex Burtin is at your side.

And as Ferdy celebrated, waving bouquets of flowers to the crowds at the Parc des Princes velodrome, he whispered into the ear of friend and cycling writer Walter Jacob: "You know what, the best is yet to come. Tomorrow, I'll see my son André, and he'll welcome me with his arms open wide."

1951

THE BATTLE OF THE TWO K'S

A Coppi-sized cloud hang over the start of the 1951 edition of the Tour de Suisse. Now positioned in between the two Grand Tours of Italy and France, the race had attracted a number of big names looking for fitness. Two of them started with K, yet newspaper column inches were dedicated to the promise given by Fausto Coppi that he would join Hugo and Ferdy on the start line in Zürich on the 15th June and the subsequent withdrawal of that promise once he realised he had also signed a contract for a race in Turin on the Tuesday evening. You can't do both, he was advised, so do the one you've legally committed yourself to doing.

The absence of Coppi allowed Alfredo Martini to stretch his legs on the first stage, attacking the peloton 100km from home and stretching his advantage at one stage to 13 minutes. Martini was no slouch. He had finished third in last year's Giro behind Hugo and was a capable climber. He had perhaps calculated that an early attack might be worthwhile given the marking taking place within the group. All eyes were on the two K's, Koblet and Kübler, and the Italian team in particular took great delight in ensuring that neither man could escape the clutches of the peloton. One Swiss rider, Giovanni Rossi, did escape but could only claw back a handful of minutes on Martini who climbed the dusty, gritty Siglistorf and then the Boertzberg with relative ease on his way to an imposing first stage win.

The second stage from Aarau to Basel was up and down, yet ridden at an infernal pace. This was led by the two rather impatient K's who took up a sizeable amount of the work on behalf of their teams to try and instil some urgency in the race. Martini punctured 12km from the end, which gave Ferdy the chance to attack and take the first half of the day's racing. The second half was a time-trial between Basel and Boncourt, and predictably Hugo won it with a comfortable 2'53" advantage over Ferdy who looked tired and drawn – perhaps due to his efforts in the Ardennes Classics not so long ago. Martini went on to lose 12 minutes over the afternoon and, in the process, his yellow jersey. Nobody really talked about Martini, though – it was all about the grace and splendour of Hugo Koblet and how he could maintain an average speed of 41.7km per hour on a course that required frequent changes of speed with punchy climbs and sharp corners, and of how he made everyone else look like donkeys.

Hugo's teammate Dino Rossi was now in yellow, so it was only normal that on the fourth stage, when escaping from the pack with Ferdy and the two Italians Fornara and Rossello – Hugo refused to do any work on the front. Ferdy gesticulated wildly, but Hugo gesticulated in return as if to say – well, you'd do the same. Ferdy took the mountains points on the Col de Pillon and in true gallant, gentlemanly style, Hugo refused to take part in the sprint, leaving the 30-second bonus to Ferdy.

The consensus was that Hugo would win this Tour de Suisse with something in hand. Dino Rossi was keeping the jersey warm for him, Ferdy was two and a half minutes behind, and Hugo looked imperious in the saddle.

The next stage between Lucerne and Lugano took in two fearsome climbs – the Oberalp and the Lukmanier. Hugo attacked first on the Devil's Bridge, chewing up the Oberalp in front of him with little apparent effort. From the lush greens of the valley below, specks of snow lay scattered among the grass verges and gradually grew in frequency until there was more white than green and soon huge banks of snow were piled either side of Hugo who rode serenely down a glistening corridor. The pass had only been opened a few days previously and Hugo gratefully accepted a newspaper to put down his jersey before taking on the descent. Of course, the descent had been cleared last of all, and this meant that layers of grit and dirt had built up. Hugo punctured shortly after the peak of the Oberalp and waited in vain for his team car, stuck further down the mountain on the other side. With frozen fingers, he put to repairing the puncture himself before climbing on and puncturing again. Rossello coasted by and then Ferdy behind him before Hugo punctured again. And again. And again.

Within time, Hugo found himself seven minutes behind Ferdy and rode as if he had lost all interest in the race.

Ferdy and Rossello both punctured on the Lukmanier but ploughed on expecting further punctures through the dust and the pebble stones. Rossello waited for Ferdy while he repaired his wheel, and as a mark of gratitude, Ferdy allowed Rossello to cross the line first at the finish line much to the ire of Race Director Carl Senn who pointed his fat finger in Ferdy's face, accusing him of selling the race.

So what exactly did happen to Hugo? Left alone on the descent of the Oberalp, we only have his version of the story, that he punctured a total of seven times and was left alone without a team car. What's more, he lost his pump, having to claim one from an eager young rider who had climbed the mountain that morning to watch his heroes. Ferdy immediately disputed Hugo's version, telling journalists that evening:

"He left with three inner tubes on his back and I can tell you right now that they were the lightest possible inner tubes, Hugo always does this. If he didn't have a team car with him – where did he find four other tubes?"

The battle of the two K's, as billed by the Swiss media, would be fought out on the final stage between Lugano and Davos. Ferdy held the yellow jersey with a lead of more than 5 minutes over Hugo. The race profile was similar to the previous day, with the Bernina and the Fluela providing a more lyrical aspect if not an easier one. Hugo attacked early on with teammate Fornara and built up a two-minute lead on the road over Ferdy whose Tebag team were working in relays to maintain the gap. Fornara had given everything for Hugo that morning, and by the time they reached the top of the Bernina Pass, Fornara was spent, dropping back to enjoy his reflection in the white lake while Hugo forged on. Those hardy souls who had made it to the top of the pass would have been able to spend a good two minutes alone watching their breath form clouds in the cold air before having the opportunity to encourage Rossello, Kübler and the rest of the peloton in their pursuit of Hugo.

And then all that was left of the Tour was the Fluela.

Some claimed that Hugo led Ferdy by two minutes at the base of the climb. Ferdy would recall that the gap was around five minutes, but you write your own legend and hope that others adopt it. The climb itself would be 13km in length, 900m in height and unrelenting. The Fluela is anything but fluent. Hugo's pace slowed dramatically every time the gradient rose above 12%, reassuming his customary grace and poise when the gradient ducked below. Ferdy had brought along Rossello and Fornara, the latter refusing to do any work while his teammate was higher up the mountain.

The gap remained at two minutes for the first half of the climb, the two K's matching each other at a distance until the lights appeared to go out in Hugo Koblet's eyes. Halfway up the Fluela, his efforts up the Bernina and through the valley between the two climbs appeared to be catching up with him. His Cilo team car pulled up alongside, but Hugo stared at the road ahead of him, mute. Leave me to it, he silently urged Dr Jan, leave me to ride and I'll get through this.

Behind, Ferdy had detached himself from the two Italians, standing on his pedals and beating out the worst of what the Fluela had to offer. On occasions, he could see the grey and red shirt of Hugo sometimes three, sometimes four hairpins ahead before banks of stone and eventually banks of snow blocked his view of his prey. Hugo looked within himself for whatever reserves he could pull upon as Ferdy pulled ever closer in his yellow jersey. Two kilometres from the summit, that lead had been cut to 55 seconds and within a further kilometre it was down to 35. When Hugo reached the summit, Ferdy was just 200m behind and another Hugo seemed to take over, sparked into life by the drop and the sight of Kübler behind him. The slow-motion chase up the Fluela mutated quickly into a high-action dash down the mountainside along the lakes and into Davos, Hugo taking aerodynamic positions into straights, Ferdy hunting him down with fits and starts of high-energy pedalling. Through the winding roads of Davos, Hugo held his lead, not that he needed to keep it, but he kept it all the same, beating Ferdy by a handful of seconds.

With a ceremonial stage into Zürich to close the Tour de Suisse, Ferdy Kübler could celebrate with relative certainty, and looking in the mirror that evening, he came to a decision that would change the rest of the season to come. He would not defend his title in the Tour de France. Some asked whether Hugo's form had left him questioning whether he could live with him – some suggested that Ferdy's weight had dropped so far that he needed some rest, to "beef up" a little. Ferdy suggested that he was just tired and he would return later in the season, perhaps for the World Championships, perhaps when Hugo was a little less hungry.

For Hugo, the Tour de Suisse was a missed opportunity but proof that he was riding well, and without the seven punctures on the descent of the Oberalp, he would have won comfortably. So he allowed Ferdy to celebrate, and he celebrated Ferdy's decision to step back from selection for the Tour de France, because now he was ready for *le Tour*.

CLIMBING TREES

There are those who would tell you that Hugo Koblet's victory in the 1951 Tour de France was guaranteed from the moment he stepped out of his Studebaker in Metz. Hindsight casts a certain inevitability on the events of this Tour, and yet Alex Burtin – waiting in the hotel lobby for his rider – knew that nothing was inevitable and that everything had to be controlled carefully. As always.

What could he control? Well, the Swiss team, for one. There would be no Ferdy Kübler, although this is no bad thing. Better to have one of the K's than both of them. Hugo is younger, more malleable, more open to suggestion. Ferdy is, well... Ferdy. But around Hugo, what did he have? Multiple Tour debutants, for a start. New names like Walter Reiser, Giovanni Rossi, Hans Sommer, Marcel Huber and, of course, Hugo himself. Not a single one of them had lined up in a Tour de France before. Alongside them, Georges Aeschlimann and the two Weilenmanns.

A lack of experience, a lack of depth, but a popular lead rider.

So there's that, at least.

The rest was out of his control. The Italians – Coppi, Bartali and Magni. They came with baggage, and plenty of it. Fausto Coppi had alighted from the train in Metz a changed man, his features drawn. His brother Serse had recently passed away after a racing accident. Fausto was welcomed in silence, riders extending handshakes, embraces and nods of sympathy. What can you say? Fausto loved his brother more than anyone in the world and yet here he was, fulfilling contractual obligations while sadness played its melancholy opera all over his face.

The French had Louison Bobet, the pre-race favourite. The chance of his life, the French press insisted. The greatest opportunity of his blossoming career. Louison was a man attending his own coronation if you were to believe the musings of Leducq, Baker d'Isy and the rest with their quills of red, white and blue. Hindsight would tell you that Louison would take time to mature and yet you always felt that at some point, there would be a new vintage. But when? 51? 52? 53? He could go on...

And here was Hugo Koblet, winner of last year's Giro d'Italia and a man in such good form that in the six pre-Tour criteriums he chose to ride, he somehow lapped his opponents in every race. Even then, people believed he would struggle in the Tour. Some were making excuses for last year's Giro, suggesting that Coppi's injury and Bartali's ageing body were to blame for Italy's failure. Some saw it as a 'blip', and that this track rider would be put in his place by a nascent Louison Bobet.

Their first lesson would come early. In the first stage, the peloton headed eastwards into headwinds and crosswinds, chasing a breakaway that included two of the minor Swiss riders, Marcel Huber and Giovanni Rossi. They found themselves alongside Apo Lazarides and Gilbert Bauvin as well, scouts sent ahead by the wily French and Italian team leaders. This was very much a breakaway day, a day for an obscure yellow jersey. And yet behind, Hugo felt it necessary to detach himself from the peloton and enjoy a 40km ride on his own, at one point cutting nearly a minute and a half from the breakaway's advantage.

How did Hugo explain this solo escapade?

"I didn't really accelerate," he told the reporter from l'Equipe. "I just found myself a bike length or two ahead of the peloton so I kept going in the hope that a few men would join me and we could launch a real counter-attack. It really wasn't up to me to ride, given that I had two men up ahead."

In the end, Hugo just wanted to see if he "had the legs", and it turned out that he did. What pleased Alex Burtin the most, and what caused the greatest amount of distress to those still in the peloton, was that Hugo wasn't really making much of an effort. He was smiling, hands on top of the handlebars. At one point he sat upright, wiped his face and then turned around to see where the peloton might be. Behind,

Magni was leading the charge, raising the pace to an alarming 50km/h. The French team had joined in too, so Alex Burtin, one eye on the speedometer in his car – chose to inform Hugo that it wasn't worth persisting and that if he rejoin the peloton, he might enjoy seeing the looks on the riders' faces.

He would also have enjoyed having the yellow jersey within the Swiss team as Giovanni Rossi took the sprint in Reims.

Hindsight, once more, gives us the impression that this was Hugo at his most imperious and that all and sundry were in awe of this Apollo-on-a-bike. Alex Burtin – when provoked – would recall that it was not always so. Other riders told reporters "Well, if he carries on like that, he won't last long", and were formulating long-game strategies on the basis that Hugo Koblet would blow early. The Giro was an aberration, Hugo is still a *pistard* who got lucky.

Worse for Alex Burtin was that Giovanni Rossi had suddenly acquired ideas above his station and was spending the evening sulking in his bedroom, muttering above his breath that the glory of his yellow jersey had been stolen by Hugo's vain escapade and that in any normal team, he would instantly have been designated team leader. Alex Burtin took a long sigh and agreed that three men would ride for Giovanni, three for Hugo, and he silently hoped that Giovanni would lose his yellow jersey as quickly as possible.

Stage 2 from Reims to Ghent in Belgium had all the ingredients of a Classic race, not least thanks to the appearance of the cobbled horror that is the

Muur de Grammont in Geraardsbergen. Hugo and Alex Burtin had agreed that not one of the race favourites should be allowed to have an "off day", which meant that Hugo had to attack early, leading the main peloton behind the day's breakaway.

Hugo attacked a total of ten times during the second stage, and at one point had to reel in Louison Bobet who must have thought "if you can't beat him, join him". The force of Hugo's attacks soon had his teammate Giovanni Rossi hanging off the back of the peloton, conceding defeat just two hours into his single day in the yellow jersey.

When Fiorenzo Magni joined the leading group, Hugo forced the pace once more. He had never climbed the Muur before, but he knew that after the bridge and the swoop into town, the cobbled climb would start to rise sharply and wend its way through the town centre. He gave no impression that he felt any harshness below his wheels, accelerating through the bends and breaking apart the group of riders that had come with him. Only the two Frenchmen, Bobet and Géminiani, could stick to Hugo's wheel as the Chapel bore into view and the gradients eased.

At the end of the day, Hugo would settle for sixth place on the stage. But his relentless behaviour was earning plaudits. Louison, for one, told reporters:

"This Swiss boy is strong and he's not afraid to attack. If we had a time trial tomorrow, he'd win by 3 minutes. But with all this effort, won't he wear himself out?"

Few had realised that this was part of Hugo's race strategy, as agreed with Alex Burtin. The Italians have brought a team of climbers, so they'll be waiting for the mountains. If you want to shake them off, you have to put them under pressure before you reach high altitude.

And so the race developed as the Tour weaved its way westwards, the yellow jersey changing hands almost daily, Hugo attacking at every opportunity and riders telling reporters they'd had enough of Hugo's attacks and that they couldn't wait for him to tire, which he surely will. For Alex Burtin, this Tour was a refreshing experience. An easier one. Complaints about money had all but disappeared – Hugo paid the team on time unlike Ferdy who needed a few nudges and curt reminders before sharing the spoils. And when Hugo was found wandering the hotel corridors in Angers, Alex Burtin flew into a panic, reminded of Ferdy Kübler's nervous anxiety. But Hugo simply wanted something to eat, so Alex Burtin took Hugo out into the streets of Angers, searching desperately for food. The only restaurant open was in the train station where Hugo ate chicken in aspic contentedly before returning to his bed where he slept contentedly. And then so did Alex Burtin.

Things are simple, Alex Burtin reflected. In the end.

The time trial could have caused any number of worries for Alex Burtin. For several hours, people were led to believe that Louison had won the stage and that Hugo had come second. Until, that was, Hugo looked at the official times and noticed a Spanish rider who had finished nearly 6 minutes behind him on the stage even though he had departed 6 minutes before him. Wait a minute, said Hugo – I overtook this guy. Something doesn't add up. The Swiss team complained to Jacques Goddet, and the mistake was found and rectified. Not only had Hugo won the time trial, he'd won it with a gap of over one whole minute on Louison Bobet. It was the fastest time trial by any rider for over two years and Hugo had achieved such a pace during the first third of the stage that he could even have been accused of taking it too easy on the descents.

There were some who even found fault in Hugo's approach to the time trial, despite his imposing win. Claude Tillet wrote for l'Equipe that Hugo had chosen a groupset perfectly adequate for climbs but wholly inadequate for the rest of the course. He even went so far as to accuse Hugo of underestimating the obvious superiority of his French and Italian rivals.

Did anything worry Hugo Koblet at all? On the surface, it appeared not. He could be found wandering around hotel kitchens, chatting genially with staff while eating ham and mayonnaise, before calmly reminding an anxious Alex Burtin that all is well, everything is allowed, even mayonnaise, and returning to his room where he would shave his legs while whistling cheerily and returning to the lobby in his hotel bathrobe to sign autographs for the girls who had been waiting since early morning to catch a glimpse of this simply gorgeous Swiss rider their fathers had been discussing. *Le Bel Hugo*, they called him.

Only one thing did worry Hugo. To be precise: one person. Fausto Coppi. Alex Burtin knew that Fausto had been playing on Hugo's mind from the very first moments of this Tour, even if Fausto himself was only going through the motions. During the stage into Clermont-Ferrand, Hugo punctured twice. On each occasion, Alex Burtin leapt from his vehicle to carry out the repairs, and what did Hugo ask? Perhaps how hard Géminiani was riding at the front, hopeful of winning in front of his home crowd? Perhaps how Robic's attacks were weakening the peloton? No, Hugo's first question was – where is Fausto?

The riders had arrived in Brive ahead of the stage to Agen, only for Hugo to take Alex Burtin to one side and admit that he was suffering from haemorrhoids. OK, thought Alex Burtin. I must keep this simple. Make sure nobody knows. Above all, let's not tell the Tour Doctor, because once he knows, everyone knows. Let's not tell the team either. Maybe just the Weilenmann brothers because they're older and wiser and also, they would crawl over broken class for Hugo. Besides, Leo's sharing a room with Hugo. Let's find a local doctor and pay him a little more.

And so Alex Burtin made the calls and found that local doctor who came quickly as promised and insisted on an incision right away, pointing out the offending haemorrhoids to Alex Burtin who made his best effort to look at Hugo's exposed backside and appear as if he understood, like a bemused car owner nodding along to a mechanic. No incisions, please pack your bags, we'll find another doctor, a doctor who doesn't do incisions, preferably. Alex Burtin found another doctor, one who would provide pills to ease the pain, and ease the pain they did. Hugo slept peacefully, and not a word was spoken of the evening.

Brive-Agen, then, started with haemorrhoids and secrecy, and ended in one of the great performances of all time, a stage that would come to define Hugo Koblet's early career. It certainly wasn't supposed to be anything special. The Tour had just visited the Massif Centrale for the first time in its history; Brive-Agen was intended to be a transitional stage taking the riders from there to the Pyrenees. A chance to breathe, to coast, to enjoy the countryside at its most bucolic, exchange stories and resume hostilities a little later. A breakaway day, perhaps a peloton sprint, and the GC contenders could roll in a little later. At the start line, Sugar Ray Robinson shared jokes with the riders. Photographers laughed as he and Hugo exchanged fake punches. This would be one of those days – a nothing stage in the sunshine. Nothing to see here.

So when Hugo attacked after just 37km of the stage, only a minor French rider called Louis Deprez would go with him. The consensus was that Hugo would wear himself out, so why not let him do just that? What a preposterous idea, attacking 140km from the finish line when you're trying to win the whole race.

Louis Deprez would later tell journalists that Hugo had told him to stick to his wheel and stay there, but commented – "I would have loved to. That guy is an aeroplane."

Deprez dispensed with, Alex Burtin pulled up alongside Hugo and enquired after his health. All is well, his rider smiled. And Alex Burtin had no reason not to believe his rider. All was very well, and few could believe what they were seeing. André Leducq, writing for Miroir des Sports, was in a car that pulled up alongside the Swiss team car. "Burtin! What on earth is he doing?" he yelled, furious that the day's restful outlook had been ruined. "You're insane, Burtin! Insane!"

But Hugo was on 'one of those days'. He had made his mind up to win the stage, to shake up the peloton ahead of the mountains and to enjoy riding at what felt like his best. Behind, there was a growing realisation that the gap was not coming down, and also that luck had abandoned the peloton. Louison Bobet punctured, taking two teammates with him to pace him back to the other riders. The Italians lost a man in a fall; he needed pacing back too. Barbotin had dropped out of the group, so the French team retreated to pace him back as well. In time, there would be two pelotons and Hugo's lead would creep up to four minutes.

Through hedgerows he weaved, only losing time on exposed sections of road where the wind blew hard in his face. French, Italian and Belgian teams tried their hardest to accelerate and cut the gap down but often there would be a red jersey with a white cross in their way, blocking their route to the front.

Depictions of this stage would later portray the peloton as exhausted and bedraggled while in contrast, Hugo was serene and imperious. This does play into a myth of sorts and gives the Swiss team little credit for the work they put in preventing attacks from the main group. It also portrays Hugo as untroubled, which was far from true. With 12km to go to the finish, Hugo told Alex Burtin that he wanted to quit, that he couldn't ride another inch. For hours, he had been riding all out, on his limit.

His opponents were ready to concede. Lucien Lazarides, for one, asked after the stage if Hugo had an engine in his stomach, continuing:

"The more we chased him, the further away he got."

Louison Bobet wondered whether he shouldn't have been at the Vigorelli instead, chasing the hour record. Raphaël Géminiani said that the Tour was over unless Hugo has some kind of serious mishap, going to add that if Hugo carries on at this rate, he'd sell his bicycle.

Fiorenzo Magni reckoned that in ten years of racing, he'd never seen such an exploit, while Fausto told teammates that the only way to beat Hugo was to hope and pray that he blows up at some point, but as he's so young, he'll recover from today's effort and the Tour was likely already over.

When Hugo arrived in Agen that afternoon, he did so over two minutes ahead of the peloton, measured by his oversized stopwatch to ensure that he would be confident in the timekeeper's own numbers. A timekeeper he doesn't trust. He then welcomed home his teammates, embracing each of them before turning to the Tour's official timekeeper to compare notes.

And still, the French media found criticism in the Swiss strategy. Leducq, whose lazy day in the countryside had been turned upside down by Alex Burtin and Hugo Koblet, labelled Alex Burtin a madman for risking it all on a flat stage with a rider who may not even make it to Paris. You'll ruin him before the Pyrenees, he thundered.

Jacques Goddet was far more admiring in his column for l'Equipe:

"You broke the chains of the peloton, you laughed in the face of convention. Prudence! Save your energy! You freed yourself from the conformity and the shackles which bind today's star riders. The purity of this exploit, the unforgettable spirit of your effort. Whatever happens next, whether you have to carry the burden of this effort each day until the 29th July, the French public to whom you have offered this magnificent festival, will forever be in your debt."

Goddet went on to write what was perhaps his longest ever column for the paper, and it was all about the magnificent Hugo Koblet who was – he forgot to mention – still seven minutes back in the general classification.

The Pyrenees had indeed arrived and the initial climbs which included the Soulor came sufficiently far from the finish line that they posed no particular problem. Hugo stuck to the wheels of the Italians who barely made a move all day, while looking for attacks from Gilbert Bauvin whom he was beginning to consider a threat. The first major Pyrenean stage was stage 14, which took in the three major climbs – Tourmalet, Aspin and Peyresourde. Hugo's concerns about Fausto grew as the Italian team leader led an attack early on in the stage. Hugo punctured 3km from the top of the Tourmalet which was the sign for his opponents to make their move, perhaps unwisely using too much energy on the mountain. Hugo calmly wiped his glasses clean as Alex Burtin changed his wheel. He climbed back on, caught everyone on the descent and then left them for dead, chasing Fausto Coppi who had already started up the Aspin. For the first time in the Tour, Hugo saw Fausto smile, and it was simply because he had been caught. Perhaps Fausto simply didn't want to be alone.

The two tried to shake each other off but ultimately couldn't. They descended together into Luchon where Hugo defeated Fausto in the sprint, taking the 60 seconds' bonus and most importantly, the yellow jersey.

For the final week of racing, the Swiss team defended their jersey with Hugo riding comparatively within himself. At times, Hugo appeared to be joking around for much of the final week. People said they saw him riding up and down the promenade in Alex Burtin's jeep. Later, at the end of the time trial from Aix to Geneva, he ran into the crowd, causing mass panic and confusion until everyone realised that he was there to kiss his mother.

The riders climbed Mont Ventoux for the first time in a Tour de France, and for the first time in this Tour, Hugo appeared to weaken a little. He was fifth at the top of the mountain behind Lazarides, Bartali and Géminiani and later complained of mechanical problems, but Hugo often complained of mechanical problems when there were problems of the mind or body. Ventoux had got into a few of the riders' heads before the climb although Hugo later assured journalists that it was no more difficult than the San Bernardino.

In the end, Hugo won the Tour by over 22 minutes ahead of French rider Raphaël Géminiani who later complained that Hugo was so strong, he may as well have been climbing trees. But racing aside, 1951 was the year that Hugo Koblet charmed an entire country. The year that the French media had to concede that there was, perhaps, another way to win the Tour de France. The 1951 Tour was a circular charm offensive with everyone Hugo met falling under his spell. They spoke of the way he combed his hair while pedalling, of how he washed his face with water from his bidon before speaking to journalists, of how this perfect gentleman was the mirror image of all those guts and glory pre-war riders who slogged it out for three weeks.

Hugo was a modern rider, at ease in time trials and mountains alike, a graceful Apollo-on-a-bike who would bring the sport to new audiences. Hugo was perfect, and he would surely win this race many times over. Surely.

HUGO: I have a new car, Ferdy. A Studebaker. Oh, you'd love it, although you wouldn't pay for it would you. I know how you love American things, just like me. It's sleek, its seats are made of leather, and the speed, oh Ferdy – it's like descending the San Bernardino. The way it takes corners, the way people look at me when I drive into town.

I have a new girl, too. She's in the movies, not my kind of movies, more yours I would guess, but she's blonde and she's beautiful and wait till you see her in the Studebaker. It's like wine and cheese. The perfect combination. Can you believe that only a few years ago I was a kid riding time trials outside town and now here I am, driving to a criterium that I'm going to win, with Waltraut Haas on my arm? This life!

This life, Ferdy. It never stops. How did you cope last year? Did you know you can fit in two criteriums in a single day? So long as the towns are close enough, you can ride one at lunchtime and another in the evening, the light's still good enough. I put my yellow jersey on, let a breakaway form, haul them in with Fausto and Rik, and then I win the sprint, just as we'd organised it, like a Molière play for the masses. They lap it up! Fausto puts his arms around me and kisses me on both cheeks, we bow to the crowd, we get in our cars and we drive to our next contractual obligation, to our next hotel room, to our next girl.

The Belgian criteriums are harder, you have to let the local boys get away first, give them time to fly in front, and then you have to make it look like you're struggling, make it look like they're pushing you all the way and remember all the way round, this is lap 5, I need to be closing in by lap 6 according to the script. But right now, nothing feels hard, nothing feels unlikely – I just add another 10% to my effort and I'm over that climb and through those cobbles and – bang – I've caught them and I'm racing to the finish line, as we'd agreed, to the flowers, the girls and the big fat cheque. Oh, and I love the Belgian girls.

Tomorrow it's Italy and I have to let Fausto win, especially if I want to get out of there alive. And then Fausto has to let me win the next day, and we'll meet afterwards and we'll have a drink and a meal and at the weekend he'll take me to meet his family and we'll all talk about Gino. And then next week I'm seeing Louison in Brittany and we'll race our cars before we race our bikes, and soon I'll go to Mexico, to parties and after-parties and we'll spend the winter on the track racing each other into the ground. Omnium, Pursuit, Six Days...

I don't want this to stop, Ferdy. I never want this to stop. I could do this forever. I want the revolutions in my legs to propel me forward to more of this, to bigger races, more beautiful women, more champagne. I want to see more of the world, I want to ride every criterium and never, ever stop. Just keep the wheel turning.

RÖSLI

Rösli Kübler could not say that she hadn't been warned. Marry a cyclist, they said; marry a cyclist and you'll not see your husband until October. Even then he'll be away on his bike and if you're lucky he'll get you pregnant during the off-season but then you'll be bringing up babies while he's riding around another country. Marry a cyclist and you might as well wait until he's 36, and you? You'll be past it.

But Rösli knew what she had signed up to. She met Ferdy while he was convalescing at his brother's home in 1940 after one of his many accidents, this time in a cyclocross event. She had gone with Hanni Minder, whose mother owned the greengrocer's in Adliswil, and couldn't help but notice Hanni's fluttering eyelashes every time Ferdy spoke, how Ferdy took care to speak to both of them equally, to look them both in the eyes. She could tell, cyclist or no cyclist, he was a good man. But Hanni was beautiful and blonde, and all cyclists liked blondes, or at least so Rösli was told.

Hanni's interest cooled the moment her mother yelled at her for even considering courting a cyclist. He's penniless that boy, I know his father, I know where he comes from. He'll come to nothing, and besides – what sort of a career is riding a bicycle anyway?

Rösli Ellenberger's mother had an altogether different opinion. In Ferdy, she saw a boy of impeccable morals, so she invited him to dinner where she encouraged the two to develop a relationship. Before long, Mrs Ellenberger had even cleared a bedroom and invited young Ferdinand to recover from his injuries in the Ellenberger household. From that moment, Rösli was Ferdy's and Ferdy was Rösli's, and always would it be.

Summers came and summers went with Ferdy in and out of the family home in Adliswil. Winters would be spent up in Arosa unless Ferdy felt the need to return to the track and make some money to get them through the season, which he often did. Life as a cycling wife didn't always suit Rösli, but she resolved herself to the cadences of the road and track seasons.

The summer of 1951, however, was materially different. Instead of riding the Tour de France, Ferdy had elected to stay at home after a difficult spring and early summer's racing. If she were honest, Ferdy could have raced the Tour, but he had chosen not to because he didn't want to ride either for or against Hugo Koblet. Ferdy never said this openly, not even to Rösli, but she knew that Hugo's performance in the Tour had stirred something in her husband. She'd find him in the afternoon, ear to the radio, listening through the static, poring over the morning papers for any sign of Hugo cracking, a sign that Hugo might be fallible. But Hugo wasn't fallible that year and avoiding the Tour would be a wise move.

Rösli sat with Ferdy for long hours, listening as he cursed Hugo, predicting with confidence that he would blow on the next stage, that this level of form is not humanly possible over three weeks. She would watch him leap from his armchair and attack his bicycle after each stage, replacing the chain, tightening the brake cables, adjusting the seat. Nothing needed doing, Ferdy just wanted to take his mind off the fact that Hugo was winning the Tour, his Tour, the Tour that he had won last year and now everyone was talking about Hugo, *Hugo Nationale*, conqueror of France.

And then she would wake with him every morning at 4:30 as he carried out his morning routine of stretches at the end of the bed. His grunts as he lifted his weights. She would prepare his breakfast of eggs and ham while he ran in the forest, returning at 5:30 to scoff everything she had made before he departed for a full day on the bicycle. Then she'd wash up and prepare breakfast for André before he woke, wash the linen, go to the market for some fresh vegetables for evening supper, maybe read a little and wait for her husband to come home.

Every other day, this was Rösli's routine throughout the summer of 1951. Ferdy would return around 4pm, peel his sweaty body from the bicycle and then she would ask where he had been. Every day it was the same. Up to the Klausen Pass – an update on the state of the roadworks – occasionally a stop at the café, a kind word from the workers before climbing the Glarus, into Altdorf, and then back round into Adliswil. The route never differed but the details sometimes did. Once, Ferdy picked up a local newspaper and discovered that alongside the many columns about Hugo, there was a mention of Ferdy Kübler – the headline read: "Ferdy wants to buy the Klausen Pass!" and together they laughed.

An hour later, Harry Herzig, Zürich's finest *soigneur* since Paul Eppstein, would be round for a full body massage. Nobody warned Rösli that marrying a cyclist meant she would have to welcome Harry Herzig and the rest of Ferdy's entourage at all times of day and night. Marry a cyclist, you marry the men around the cyclist. *Soigneurs*, doctors, medics, charlatans, juju men, all with their suspicious bags and surreptitious glances. Ferdy never touched even so much as a vitamin pill but she knew what they were touting and she knew the world her husband was navigating.

She would clean up after dinner while an exhausted Ferdy read to André and she would try to guess which of them would fall asleep first. André would chuckle – Daddy, you go to bed with the chickens, and Ferdy would be in bed by 7:30, out like a light.

Rösli had signed up to this. She was under no illusions. Her role was not just to run the household, not just to feed her husband and look after his physical needs. Her role had expanded over the years. She knew her husband was coming towards the end of his racing years, that the legs would eventually give out and that Hugo would go on for years, winning races while her husband eased himself into his slippers. Her role would be to nudge Ferdy in the right direction, to agree with what he wanted her to agree to, to gently shape the end of his career and help him come to terms with Hugo's growing popularity.

It was Rösli who agreed, and therefore rubber-stamped Ferdy's decision not to take part in any major races ahead of the World Championships.

The worlds, he had said to her in June. I'd love to win the Worlds.

Well, she replied – you already have a bronze and a silver. A gold would go very nicely, wouldn't it?

This had perked him up. Got him sitting up straight in the armchair. Yes, a gold medal would go very nicely. I've won a Grand Tour. I've won Classics. I've won the Tour de Suisse... if I could win the Worlds, I'd be one of the greats, wouldn't I?

You already are one of the greats, my dear, she would reply, and he would quieten down, thinking of how he could win the Worlds. Of how he could beat Fausto, Hugo, Gino, Louison, Fiorenzo, all of them, if he could dedicate his summer to preparing for this one race. He could sacrifice the criteriums, well – most of them... the stage races too, the meat and potatoes of the road cycling calendar. They'd have to tighten their belts. It would be a gamble and if he were to lose, he would have to spend the winter racing track events to make up the difference, risking his ageing body for a payday.

Rösli felt the weight of her acquiescence every morning Ferdy left for the Klausen Pass, and when time came for Ferdy to leave for Varese, she felt that tightness in her chest that she hadn't felt since Hanni Minder's mother told her that cyclists could ruin your life.

FERDY: *There wasn't a single day before Varese where I didn't ask myself, Ferdy – what are you doing? I had turned down criteriums from three different countries, avoided the Tour de France, and I had barely entered a competitive race for two months. My merchant's heart was pounding with fear – had I made the wrong move? Was I giving everything up for a roll of the dice?*

Rösli though, she knew me better than anyone. Ferdy, she would say, you've won two medals already, but I know you want the gold medal. You can do it.

I remember these days as clearly as any race, Hugo. I would wake super early, around 4:30 in the morning and do some stretches before going for a run in the forest. When I returned, my breakfast would be on the table – usually eggs or whatever Rösli could find at the market – and then I would ride for many hours, every time the same route, out of Adliswil to Altdorf, over the Klausen Pass and the Glarus and back home for late afternoon.

You know, they were still repairing the Klausen Pass at that point. The workmen were surprised when I rode through the first time, and the next time they called out to me. After the first week they shouted "Ferdy wants to buy the Klausen Pass!" and the next day it was in the local newspapers that I was to be seen training every day here. A few local people even came out to cheer me on and that really kept me going.

Rösli would greet me every evening as I came home. She'd have that smile on her face, that smile that all cyclists' wives have whenever a broken, sweaty man removes himself from his bicycle and slumps into whichever chair is nearest, and she'd bring me a drink and some raw eggs. André would come running over. At this age, he was just beginning to string some sentences together, I always remember him asking if I was going to sleep with the chickens, and I would always laugh and we'd read something together before I fell asleep around 7, every night wondering what am I doing, why am I doing this crazy thing for just one race, one single race. But I felt myself getting stronger.

You do know, of course you know, that I rode that race against one man and one man alone. The

Belgians thought we were stupid having two Swiss teams with two team leaders. Rik the first came over to me before the race and said "I don't care which of you wins, but can you keep the rest of us out of it?" and I did laugh at that, and I still do to this day.

You worried the life out of me before that race, Hugo. All that I had given up, and it was still a gamble that I could somehow beat my own teammate to the World Championships. All I could do was prepare myself for this race, but I couldn't prepare what you might do that day. This was always the great unknown for me.

On Friday 31st August, Rösli and her husband packed the car and left for Lugano via the Gotthard pass. It was a sultry day at first, the kind of day when most people would drive with the windows down. Ferdy insisted on keeping the windows up for fear of catching a cold. Of this, she had been warned. Cyclists, they said, are always afraid of the slightest breeze. A mere sniffle will send them into a nervous breakdown. At the top of the Gotthard pass, the temperature was down to single figures, so Ferdy stopped the car and jumped out.

"What now, Ferdy?" asked poor Rösli, stepping gingerly out of the car and rubbing her bare arms to get warm.

164

"I need my thermals," he replied, rummaging through the boot.

Rösli got back in the car and waited, staring coldly out at the lonely mountains. A wind whipped up. She pulled her cardigan in closer to her. Ferdy crumpled himself back into the car, thermals on his lap and haphazardly re-dressed himself, mumbling to himself – this is better, much better, you see Rösli, I can't risk getting cold. Not today. Not after all this work.

In Lugano, Ferdy checked Rösli's hotel bedroom and kissed her goodbye, jumping on his bicycle and riding into Varese alone to the Croci-Torti household. Signora Croci-Torti was making minestrone and fillet of beef with rice, while her husband Emilio was receiving a massage from Italo Villa, the renowned Milanese *soigneur*. In the corner of the room, Dr Max Mettler was pretending to read a newspaper and Alex Burtin was on his way with an update on team selection. Team Ferdy, however, was almost complete.

While Ferdy was locked in the Croci-Tortis' spare bedroom, under strict orders to sleep at least ten hours by both Villa and Mettler, Alex Burtin was shuttling between hotel rooms and apartments trying to negotiate his final team of six. Or, to be precise, his final two teams of three. Hugo Koblet was staying locally and would rely on Gottfried Weilenmann as his support. Fritz Schär was a moderate – a rare thing these days, and the Italian-speaking contingent were insistent upon Giovanni

Rossi – another neutral of sorts. The French speakers mystifyingly called for Fritz Zbinden, and Marcel Huber had been on the phone asking to ride for Hugo.

There were further complications when Fritz Schär failed to register on time, so Alex Burtin opted to speak to Ferdy to ask him who he preferred, given that Schär could have been persuaded to ride for him, but he was turned away at the door by Dr Mettler. But it's only 7pm, Alex Burtin insisted, only to be met with a firm "I know" from the doctor, and a curt "please come back in the morning". Not even the to and fro of the Swiss team selection was enough for them to wake Ferdy up.

So what were the team orders? Gopf Weilenmann had made it clear to all and sundry that he was in Varese to work for his friend Hugo Koblet, wishing "with all his heart" that Hugo become world champion. But what if Ferdy were to attack, what if Gopf's job were to work for Ferdy in the "national interest". Hugo soothed his nerves – if Ferdy attacks, then our job is to slow the peloton down. Just as he would for me, no? And if he rides against me, then we ride 100% against Ferdy. Simple.

In her hotel bedroom just over the border in Switzerland, Rösli awoke alone for the first time in what felt like a lifetime, and she felt powerless.

THE WORLDS

Ferdy Kübler woke on the morning of the 1951 World Championships at the urging of Dr Mettler. Ferdy, Ferdy, today is a tough race, you really do have to wake up right away. It took him a couple of seconds to get his bearings. A single bed. A wall on the wrong side. Whose rug is this? Why is this moustache in my face telling me to get out of this strange bed?

From the kitchen, the smell of home-cooked food. Eggs, ham, fresh bread... Signora Croci-Torti was preparing breakfast, her husband washing his face while singing in the bathroom. Outside Ferdy's window, disparate voices of different nationalities were singing the names of different riders, mostly Bartali, occasionally Hugo, occasionally Ferdy. A hocking of phlegm for van Steenbergen.

Ferdy rose, politely greeted his host's wife and politely waited before being asked to sit down by Signora Croci-Torti. Emilio, his loyal friend of many years, heartily *ciao*-ed Ferdy and slapped him on the back while Dr Mettler removed Ferdy's plate for inspection. Outside the front door, Alex Burtin was nervously pacing up and down on the landing. He had been turned away the previous evening and had spent half the night wondering how on earth to strategise a race in which he effectively had two teams to manage. Should he back one of the teams? Should he find a way to back both of them? Why does everything have to be so complicated? And given the fact that the smell of eggs and fresh bread is permeating through the door of the Croci-Tortis, shouldn't he finally pluck up the courage to knock on it?

Varese had collectively awoken to bright autumnal sunshine after a night of storms. Outside the Croci-Torti windows, the *tifosi* of many nationalities were hurrying to find vantage points. Nationalities came with differing, often regional, loyalties. The Italians had Bartali and Magni as well as Minardi and Bevilacqua to make up for the absence of Fausto Coppi. The French had Bobet and Géminiani. The Belgians had too many names to mention, but they were names that were scrawled, along with others, on the roads, draped on sheets out of windows and chanted from the already heaving café terrasses.

The race would leave Varese at 9am, taking in a 24.6km loop that would flirt with the Swiss border into Fogliaro, Rasa, Brinzo and Bedero before heading back into the city centre via Minera and Valganna. It would return a further eleven times, covering a gruelling 295km in total. The climbs are minor compared to the Alpine tests you would encounter further west or to the north – a 130m climb into Rasa and a 1km climb around Bedero. A little ramp around Valganna would test the legs, but this was a course that was designed to grind riders down.

Each climb represented little danger in isolation but would offer opportunities for attacks, as would some of the tighter roads inside Varese itself. However, it's the nature of World Championships to put an attritional strain on the riders. Classic races are usually ridden point-to-point, allowing riders to measure their race strategy dependent on landmark or location, while a Worlds is a tightly escalating criterium-style drama, ratcheting up lap-by-lap, spitting riders out until a few hardy souls remain. Ferdy has twice been among those hardy souls, twice on the podium without taking the rainbow bands back to Adliswil.

Two years ago in Copenhagen, Ferdy had found himself between a rock and a hard place. The rock was Rik van Steenbergen, the Belgian sprinter Ferdy had beaten multiple times during the 1949 season, and the hard place was the inevitable Fausto Coppi, yet to win the rainbow jersey. To understand why Ferdy chose to back one over the other and settle for a silver medal, we have to go back to the early spring of that year.

Ferdy had come back from his winter retreat to lodge with a Swiss family in Brussels. Day after day, he would ride the cobbled *bergs* and the concrete *betonweg* with van Steenbergen and two other Belgians, the '48 World Champion Briek Schotte and Ernest Sterckx. Those days would be long and hard, their only nourishment chips and mustard from roadside kiosks. Ferdy was developing a taste for Flanders and over the coming days and weeks, Flanders would develop something of a taste for Ferdy, hollering his name in gutteral Flemish. Van Steenbergen introduced his friend to his manager, Jean van Buggenhout, who revealed a world of contracts and criteriums to the Swiss rider.

Van Buggenhout was an influential man in Belgium at least, and nurtured a rivalry with André Mouton whose stronghold was across the border in France. Mouton had one particular contract that every manager coveted – that of Fausto Coppi. Imagine then if Fausto – winner of the Tour and the Giro that year – could win the World Championships as well. Mouton could parade his rider around every venue and every town centre criterium in France, and would he need any of Van Buggenhout's riders? Unlikely.

So as Ferdy entered the final kilometres of the 1949 race, he knew that he could not let Fausto Coppi win. Often, World Championship races are won not on nationality but on contracts. Should Ferdy help van Steenbergen, he would have access to around 50 races in Belgium and Holland. That's at least 50,000 francs in entrance fees alone.

The agreement was simple enough. Van

Steenbergen would attack and Ferdy would cover. If Fausto were to escape, Ferdy would chase to slow him down. And this is how it transpired. Fausto was reeled in, van Steenbergen attacked and Ferdy dutifully blocked, giving a frustrated Fausto no room at all to manoeuvre.

As Ferdy stood celebrating his silver medal on the podium, the Swiss team manager Hans Martin knew that he'd been had. Ferdy had sold the World Championships for a bunch of contracts and a pile of cash, while convincing his manager that he was riding for the win. Hans Martin left his role soon after, blaming Ferdy for losing both the Tour and the Worlds in the same year.

There was little doubt the next year in Moorslede when Briek Schotte won the rainbow bands back in his beloved Flanders. Ferdy followed up in third place with little suspicion that he had sold the race, and the Flandrien public chanted his name with every lap of the course. Nobody was beating Briek Schotte that year.

But in Varese, Ferdy had made his intentions quite clear. There are no deals to be struck, he is here to win. And yet, there is always Hugo Koblet.

For days, Alex Burtin has been shuttling between two camps as mediator. His entire team selection was based around who would race for whom and was only decided in the final hours. The two K's were barely acknowledging each other, never mind on speaking terms, so Alex Burtin did the talking for them. Hugo didn't want Ferdy in the race at all, he wanted a team based around himself because that's what you do when you have the Tour de France winner in your team. Alex Burtin would have agreed, but what can you do – Ferdy is fit, Ferdy wants to race. You can't negotiate with a hungry Ferdy Kübler.

Well, OK, some people can.

Riders mostly coalesced around Hugo, and Hugo could even find friends within the international community, should he ask for them. Ferdy is a little harder to like. Riders know that he needs a nudge when it comes to payments, and he's probably on the take with someone else. Only Emilio Croci-Torti stays loyal to Ferdy.

So an agreement – if not a deal – is tentatively struck between the two K's. Whoever looks most likely to win gets the support of the other.

This meant that on the first lap, when Hugo escaped, Ferdy found himself in the role of reluctant *domestique*, marshalling the peloton and protecting the breakaway from any surprise attacks. Worse, Hugo's best friend Gottfried Weilenmann was breathing down Ferdy's neck, making sure he was on his best behaviour. Mind your place here, Kübler... my man is up the road.

This puts Ferdy in a difficult position. His role is not to attack Hugo, but to appear to be managing the gap, to appear to be working on Hugo's behalf. If Hugo were later to discover that Ferdy had been leading the chase behind, who knows how he would react later on. It would be a long day in the saddle.

Hugo had gone ahead with Géminiani, Voorting, Kerkhove and the German rider Schwarzer. It was almost a full hand of nations, so each team had responsibilities to keep the gap within that Goldilocks zone – not too close, but not too far that it couldn't be chased down if support were needed. The only nation not involved was the Italian team, who appeared to be keeping the powder dry. For now.

Emilio and Ferdy took to the front to manage the group and maintain the balance, but mostly to avoid raising suspicion.

Hugo's escape only lasted a couple of laps though. By lap three, Hugo appeared to be fading and had fallen back into the main pack. Ferdy instantly saw his opportunity to attack, leaving Hugo in the group and joining Emilio and ten others.

Weilenmann asks Hugo for instructions and is told to work for Ferdy, to manage the group and to ensure that nobody gets away. He pleads for a more aggressive strategy, but Hugo shakes his head. Ferdy worked for me, so I will work for Ferdy was the response.

At the front, Ferdy looks around and sees no van Steenbergen, no Magni, no Bobet. The gap goes up to two minutes, then three and then four minutes. This might be the move, he thinks. A further lap goes by and Ferdy talks to himself – Ferdy come on, Ferdy you're a pilgrim, Ferdy you're responsible for your own fate. But attacks will come, there is still time.

On the sixth lap, a crescendo goes around, and Ferdy can pick out individual voices in the crowd: Magni's coming! Magni's coming! *Arriva Magni!* The loudspeakers around the course echoed the words – Fiorenzo Magni is on his way.

From nowhere, Magni had broken free from the second group marshalled by Koblet and Weilenmann and was tearing up the course with an expression of ferocious determination. Emilio Croci-Torti dropped back to find him and was surprised to find Magni not four minutes behind but just a few hundred metres. He pulled in front of Magni, pretending to take turns but the rampaging Italian flew past the tiring Croci-Torti, leaving him for dead. Magni's effort was huge; at one point he was nearly six minutes down on the lead group and within 45 kilometres, he was within it.

More Italians were splitting from the pack and finding their way to the front. Minardi had been there from the start – the scout sent ahead by the bigger fish, the viper in our nest. Magni is now with Kübler, refusing to take turns on the front as he recovers from his effort. Bevilacqua has bridged the gap and the resulting cacophony in the centre of Varese amplifies with each lap as the Italian strategy is revealed.

With three laps to go, Ferdy is managing his resources, doubting his ability to counter the three Italians. What if there were more? There were rumours flying around the group that Bartali was on his way. Could it get any worse? He thought Minardi was the scout, but what if the other two were scouts as well, all slowing him down so that Gino Bartali could spring up at the last minute and pinch glory from him? The name Bartali starts to ring round the course, from Varese to Ganna to Brinzo and Bedero. It's no longer about Magni, it's about the attack from the old man, the rider who gets better the longer he's in the saddle.

Bartali had indeed broken away from the group, but finds himself with one man – Hugo Koblet. Hugo may not be on his best day, but Gino doesn't know that. Together they relay, Bartali believing that Hugo wants Ferdy beaten, Hugo trying to slow Bartali down.

"Hey Hugo", Bartali shouts over his shoulder. "You know what they'll say about you if Ferdy wins this race?"

Hugo feigns disinterest.

"No? Nothing? Well, I'll tell you. They'll say that he's the greatest rider in Switzerland. That you couldn't keep up with him. Ha! How do you like that?"

If this were meant to encourage Hugo, to chivvy him into action to support Bartali, it had failed. Hugo slowed to a standstill and climbed from his bike, watching Gino's gesticulations as he rode away, alone. Do it all yourself, thought Hugo. You'll never make it now.

Hugo's summer had taken its toll, but he had done his work today.

Bartali had started 6 minutes down on the lead group. With Hugo, he had cut it down to four minutes.

Without Hugo, he had found a further two, but time was running out for Gino despite the urging of the partisan crowds of Varese. However hard Gino tried, however much Magni and the team attempted to put the brakes on the front group, a gap remained. With one lap to go, the bell rings and Ferdy seeks out the blackboards once more.

Bartali is just twenty seconds back.

Find a straight road, and if you dare look back, you would see Gino Bartali. But you would also see a road just one metre wide, fans having broken through the barriers, cars struggling to get through, motorbikes forcing people to give room. As hard as Gino Bartali tried, there was precious little room into which he could accelerate. The irony, thought Bartali. These people want me to win, but they're stopping me.

The sun had disappeared behind the haze, heat rising from the streets. Spectators five, sometimes ten-deep, decked out in impromptu hats made from newspapers bearing the legs and machinery of the riders, roared the lead group on. From this moment, Ferdy's whole world is the narrow ribbon of road that snakes and twists through Varese and out into the countryside, the only inhabitants of this world himself and the handful of men who have gone with him. Magni, bald and wide-shouldered, unusually quiet alongside his compatriots Minardi and Bevilacqua. He would be their leader, surely, in the absence of Bartali, but Ferdy reckoned that in this new world of theirs, they would abandon all pretence and all would want the rainbow bands.

And this German Schwarzer, who is he? What is he capable of? He is the unknown, the chaos.

Ferdy's mind was racing. The calculations. The pitfalls. Don't puncture now. Just watch the road, avoid the spectators, keep going and follow any attacks, but most of all, don't lose it on a technicality. After all those days riding the Klausen Pass, all those early mornings and all this preparation.

Magni attacked first. It was up to Ferdy to bring him back, sit on his wheel and put a halt to his escapade. Bevilacqua then tackled a descent at high speed, opening up a 200m gap which only Ferdy could close. No sooner had Ferdy closed the gap on one Italian, another attacked – Minardi this time. Then Magni. The Italians had no strategy other than to wear Ferdy down, to toy with him like a pack of dogs and then to fight it out between themselves. But their time was running out. Ferdy thought about attacking on the final climb but made a choice – to place confidence in his sprint. They have, after all, used up their energy attacking me. It's down to who has the energy.

The crowds had been ushered back behind the barriers for the final kilometre. The road had widened and the leading group spread out, looking for a racing line. And now – at this final, desperate moment, Fiorenzo Magni offered a deal. "How much do you want?" In previous years, Ferdy would have shouted a figure or an arrangement of some description, but his response – as quick as a sprint – was *"non posso, voglio vincere"* – I can't, I want to win.

Almost as quickly, the Italians lined themselves up. Minardi first, Bevilacqua second, Magni on third wheel. Magni had struck his deal with his own teammates. Ferdy took Magni's wheel almost on instinct. 400 metres before the line, Minardi dropped off. Bevilacqua took it a further 300 metres. Ferdy needed to get the drop on Magni, to find that fraction of a second where he could get the acceleration in first. He found a gap on the right-hand side and plunged into it, head first. Magni grimaced and responded, but he who responds loses and Magni knew it. Ferdy could see the line, Magni was beaten. There was no one else. No one in the world could beat him now.

He had time to smile, to loosen his toe clip and pass the line – champion of the world.

FERDY: *When did I learn about what you did in the '51 Worlds? It certainly wasn't on the day, and it certainly wasn't on the streets of Ticino the evening of the race.*

I was lost in the celebrations, lost in the replays of the race in my mind. For days, maybe weeks, I was celebrating not a victory over Magni, but a victory over you. I was obsessed that summer, Hugo. Listening to you on the radio, reading about you every day, I wasn't just obsessed with beating you, I was obsessed with the possibility that I might

*not win anything ever again. That Ferdy Kübler
would be just another name in the history books
that nobody speaks of, while everyone talks about
Hugo Koblet.*

*I spent an entire summer riding myself into peak
fitness for this one race with your name nagging
at me constantly. Rösli kept telling me to let it go,
to see you as my successor, not my competitor, but
stubborn old Ferdy would never let it go, not this
year and not for many years.*

*Of course, it might all have been very different
if Gino Bartali had made it to the front group. He
would have had three Italians working for him, I
don't think I'd ever have found room for a sprint, or
even room to respond to an attack.*

*He told me later what he said to you, how he tried
to shame you into riding against me, how you had
slowed him down for a whole lap until he got so
frustrated, he had to double his effort to lose you.*

*You were my doping that year, Hugo, but I often
wonder – if we could win the Worlds without
talking to each other, what could we have done if
we had spoken?*

1952

THERE IS A LIGHT
THAT SEEMS
TO HAVE GONE OUT

If you look at Hugo Koblet, he is to all intents and purposes the same man as he was last year. The hairline may have receded a millimetre or two, but the good looks remain. The muscles are more or less the same, too. The tan lines have, if anything, deepened. But look closer, look at the eyes and where last year there was a light, this year there is nothing. What light there was has been extinguished. In its place, a void. At times, a tear.

The fork in the road, the point at which Hugo, casting his mind back, had taken the wrong direction – was in last year's Tour de France. It had all seemed too easy, it was all going too well. The men from Mexico had sought him out, pressed the flesh, charmed the *pedaleur de charme*. The Tour was almost beyond doubt at that point, Hugo the winner-elect. Would he like to visit Mexico, they asked. There's a Tour, not like this Tour, a young Tour, not quite as many stages, we could do with some glitter, a little stardust. Who better than the man everyone says is going to dominate cycling for many years to come, the man with film-star looks? Simply turn up, wave, cut a ribbon at the start line. Like Orson Welles, but more athletic.

Hugo never can say no.

Winning the Tour de France came with more than just a trip to Mexico, though. There were criteriums to be raced around France and Belgium. Many of them came with a script to be played out, parties to be attended, girls to be met. There were visits to the bike factory, contractual ones. Look at some frames, point admiringly for the photographers, shake some hands. There was the Swiss National Road Race, but that went to Ferdy, who else, and then the Track Championships too. He punctured in the Pursuit, but he was tired so he didn't mind. Then there was the Grand Prix du Centenaire in Brussels in which Hugo saw off Raymond Impanis and then the World Pursuit Championships in Milan, but Antonio Bevilacqua had the advantage that day and Hugo gracefully declined the opportunity to win, or so he would say. The World Championships followed, and they went to Ferdy, who else. Hugo thought it better not to bring Gino Bartali to the front and – gentleman that he is – stepped off his bike and let Gino do the hard work himself. There was the Criterium des As at Longchamp, which Hugo won too, beating Rik van Steenbergen, Louison Bobet and Fausto Coppi, but that was only preparation for the Grand Prix des Nations, ultimately Hugo's ambition for this end-of-season rally where Hugo reached 40km/h and brought the Grand Prix home to Switzerland, ahead from start to finish. There was Paris-Tours too, which was more for show than anything else, in which Hugo escaped alone to chase down a breakaway and why not overtake the breakaway and win the whole thing himself but alas, there wasn't much left in the legs after all and he might as well save himself for Lugano and the Grand Prix Vanini, a 75km time trial. Fausto took this one, Hugo took second.

And that, you might have thought, was that. The road season was finally over, but the track season never really ends and indeed it only really gets going when the roadies end theirs. Koblet's tiredness was beginning to tell as he led a team of foreigners against a French team. They won all four rounds against the French, Hugo winning over 15km behind a motorised derny. Then there was Bergamo and a tandem with Ferdy Kübler, who else, but nobody beats Magni-Minardi on a tandem. And then there was the Criterium d'Europe at the Velodrome d'Hiver in Paris and yet another tandem match where Hugo joined up with Fausto Coppi to take on the track specialists Roger Godeau and Raymond Goussot. Another defeat, but the coffers were filling up and Hugo knew he'd recover soon enough, especially if he could ride with his best friend Fausto. And he'd be on holiday soon, feet up on a Mexican beach, relaxing in hotel bedrooms and who knows, relaxing with some Mexican girls in a hotel bedroom.

The first days in Mexico did not disappoint. Hugo was welcomed like a prince. Garlands were hung around his neck, flowers laid at his feet, the most beautiful Mexican girls draped around his shoulders. From Veracruz to Tampico and Aguascaliente, it was party after party, girl after girl, drink after drink, meal after meal. Life as a Tour de France winner was beginning to suit Hugo Koblet.

Until the day they asked Hugo to ride one of the stages of the Tour of Mexico. Show us what you're made of, they said. Show the people of Mexico the beautiful Hugo Koblet. Leave 30 minutes ahead of the riders, a sort of one-man *caravane publicitaire*, soak up the adulation on the roads of Mexico. Except that once Hugo Koblet left the start line, the crowds dried up and the streets were parched, cracked and dusty. The country roads threw Hugo from left to right; his legs seized up. All artistry had been left behind, Hugo was just another pedal-turning foreigner, lost in a foreign land. He had been riding almost non-stop since spring, cashing in on his newfound fame and status, never stopping to relax or rest, never stopping to think, just riding, partying, drinking, meeting girls, eating, meeting more girls, partying, riding, winning or not winning, it didn't matter so long as it all just kept coming. Now the responsibilities of a Tour winner were made clear to him as a pedalled under the hot sun in the middle of Mexico, his only company a support car of Mexican commissaires shouting the occasional encouragement and the potential shame that he might be caught by the amateurs in that Mexican peloton.

Hugo left something on those Mexican roads. When he returned to Switzerland, he continued to play the role. He could be found at theatres and ski stations but he didn't quite look the same. Haggard. Coughing, they would say. Tired, very tired. Rumours flew around that Hugo had brought back a venereal disease from some Mexican girl or other, a rumour that Hugo acknowledged to his friends to be true. What was I doing, he would laugh, coughing and scratching down below and wheezing to himself. What was I doing. As the winter wore on and Hugo's illness deepened, he sought stronger and stronger medicine to hide the sickness from his friends. I'm fine, just fine, can't wait to get going again.

The 1952 season started in Algiers where a certain sluggishness could be put down to Hugo's renowned dislike for training. Milan-San Remo equally saw Hugo finish in the peloton, and he abandoned during stage 4 of Paris-Cote d'Azur after just 100km between Arles and Antibes. This was just preparation, Hugo told himself. Preparation for the Giro, the race that launched his career two years ago. Things will get better once the sickness clears, as it always does. You can prepare on the track, he noted, and he duly won the Swiss Pursuit Championships for the sixth consecutive time, this time after coming 2nd in the Tour de Romandie. Yet still, the wheels turned with less ease than last year; at times, the machine felt alien to Hugo. Occasionally, he felt as if he'd forgotten how to ride a bike. Occasionally, he felt his old self again.

Hugo lurched from stage to stage in the Giro d'Italia. In the time trial between Bolzano and Como, Hugo lost 15 seconds to Fausto Coppi and with each day, the legs lost their lustre and by the time of the second time trial between Roma and Rocca di Papa, he finished over three minutes behind Coppi. He found it hard to accept that the race was passing him by, each day trying to force a little more out of the legs that had propelled him to victory two years ago, the legs that only 9 months previously were demoralising his competition in the Tour de France. Hugo wondered whether things would ever get easier. Long days in the saddle, riding through valleys and mountain passes, banks of snow, with no sense of improvement or purpose, no sense that he could ever reach Coppi. Worse, that Coppi had moved forwards while he had moved backwards.

Perhaps the Giro is just preparation for the Tour de France, and before that, the Tour de Suisse would be ideal for fine-tuning his form.

That Tour de Suisse left Zürich on the 14th June and was billed as a re-match of the 1951 duel of the two K's. Hugo found a little hope on the early stages, finishing third on the stage from Basel to Le Locle, and then fifth the following day as the race finished in Adelboden. Hugo and Ferdy were watching each other, sending riders to mark every move. The next stage from Adelboden to Monthey, the weather turned and so did Hugo's health. The sickness had returned as the rain seeped through Hugo's clothing. Through the cold, moist mountain air, Hugo struggled to propel his machine forwards. His body convulsed as he coughed and the bike shook with him. Every effort would bring about another retching and coughing fit, but Hugo made it to the finish line, which was an achievement in itself.

At night, Hugo could barely sleep. Having barely eaten, he tossed and turned, drenching his bedsheets with sweat and tears. Hans Martin was called to Hugo's side and immediately called for the Tour doctor, only to find he wasn't available. So he called an ambulance, and Hans Martin's worst fears were realised – Hugo was suffering from the same sickness as Hans Martin's wife – a kidney infection. The doctor gives Hugo an injection and he is told to sleep as long as possible.

He woke late, his eyes red, asking to abandon the race.

HUGO: *I lost ten years of my career in one single morning, Ferdy. I went from a rider in his prime to a rider past his best in the blink of an eye. They assassinated me.*

Carl Senn was in the room, his fat fleshy fingers counting the cash, insisting I continue. For the good of the Tour de Suisse, for the good of cycling, you must continue, he kept saying. You can't give up on the Tour de Suisse Hugo dear boy. The Tour de Suisse would never give up on you! And there was Doctor Gossweiler too, with his bag of tricks.

Turn on your side, Hugo, he said – we'll give you some vitamins to help you through the day. This kidney infection you speak of, you can get through it.

Nobody asked me whether I wanted to get through it. I just wanted to sleep, to stay in bed and to leave the season behind me. I would have been happy to stay there until winter if they'd let me.

Vitamins, they said.

I remember every detail of that morning. I've replayed it over and over in my mind. Sometimes, I turn over and kick Doctor Gossweiler in the face. Sometimes I grab the needle from his hand and slam it straight into Carl Senn's fat neck and I watch him die. Usually, I just lie there immobile, compliant, and I let them do it again and again as the sheets swallow me whole.

I turned over and I let them assassinate me, and that was the beginning of the end. The liquid entered my bloodstream and found its way around my body, not once did I question what the liquid might be. I trusted them, and they broke me.

On seeing Hugo Koblet on the start line at Monthey for the time trial up to Crans, journalists were up in arms. Walter Grimm chased down Hugo's personal doctor Eugen Rupf and ask what on earth had possessed Hugo to start the day. Dr Rupf replied that he had nothing to do with it, that Carl Senn had rejected Hugo's request to withdraw from the race. According to a number of sources, Dr Rupf had given his opinion that morning – for Hugo to pack his bags immediately and return home.

Just what did they put in Hugo Koblet's back that morning? It most certainly wasn't vitamins and was most likely amphetamines, most likely rather a lot of amphetamines. Some journalists claimed to have seen vials of Akzedron as proof that Hugo had been injected with the most common amphetamine of the time. For some riders, Akzedron is a choice. A risk worth taking.

The amphetamines were a sticking plaster at first. Hugo launched himself out of Monthey, almost discovering an ease in his pedal stroke that he had not felt for many months. At the foot of the climb, he was 20 seconds ahead of Pasquale Fornara, feeling the blood rush through his veins. And yet, as the road tilted upwards, Hugo fought with his bicycle, the machine underneath feeling foreign as he zig-zagged up the climb to ease out the gradient. Riders passed him, looks of concern on their faces, gesticulating back at the cars. Hans Martin drove alongside, urging Hugo to get back in the car. You're sweating Hugo – what did they give you? What have you taken?

Hugo did finish, as he insisted he would. He noticed the looks of concern on the faces of everyone around. His mother, most of all. Ferdy, who else, was the first to see Frau Koblet's discomfort at her son's condition and leapt into the crowd to hand her his bouquet and comfort her. Ferdy, who else, was the man to prop Hugo up to stop him from keeling over, who led him to a place of security, who called for the medics, who whispered Hugo what have they done to you? What have you done to yourself?

On his return to Zürich, Hugo was seen by Dr Rupf whose diagnosis was severe. Words fell from his mouth and Hugo watched them land. You've been injected with amphetamines, and it has affected your bone marrow. Your heart has expanded and your bone marrow is less active than before. Whereas once you had 5 million red blood cells, you now only have 3 million. And so on, and so on. Hugo sat and took the news in a stupor, everything was a blur. These words, they mean nothing to me Doctor. Tell me in terms I will understand. What does this actually mean? In crude terms, the Doctor replied, you'll suffer in the mountains. The thinner the air, the worse you will feel. Don't even think about mountain passes. You won't race the Tour de France, I'm forbidding you right now, and you won't even start training until July at the very earliest. If I catch you on a bike, I'll be straight on the phone to your mother.

Hugo quickly skitted from grief to denial, announcing his intention to get on the train right away for Brest and start the Tour de France against the advice of his doctors.

The pieces had already been written, though. Jacques Goddet had eloquently lamented the absence of the beautiful Hugo from his Tour in l'Equipe. Alex Burtin had already left him out of the squad but Hugo was making plans to fly into France, at the very least to meet his teammates as they arrive in Mulhouse. The effort was too much though; Hugo didn't make it to France. He didn't leave home.

After denial came reason. He accepted that the pain in his kidneys was not going to disappear, so he took up an invitation to Davos where he would stay with a friend for a week on a farm, sleeping 12 hours a day, going to bed with the chickens and waking with the cows. There would be Tours aplenty in the future, so why hurry, why rush into a hasty Tour when all was obviously not well. The body is young and the kidneys will heal. Why not wait until the August criteriums.

And so Hugo retreated to Egyptian cotton bedsheets and early nights and the weeks and months went by in a bucolic haze.

As 1952 wore on, Hugo gained weight and left the bicycle in the shed. There were time trials scheduled, but none went ahead, at least for Hugo. He did ride the Criterium des As at Longchamp, but that is perhaps best left unmentioned. Instructed by Dr Rupf to restrain his efforts to at most 80% of his capability, Hugo saw little point in making even that much effort. After all, if you can't ride to your maximum, why ride at all?

Why ride at all, he would mouth to himself silently in the mirror. Why ride at all. If I'm not the same rider, how come I look the same. A little rounder, a little heavier, but I'm still Hugo Koblet and girls still ask for my photograph.

But if Hugo Koblet can't ride to his maximum, then what becomes of Hugo Koblet?

PUNCH-UPS AND FADE-OUTS

The question on Ferdy Kübler's lips at the start of the 1952 was how to make the most of Ferdy Kübler. After all, as Rösli keeps reminding him, there's only so much Ferdy Kübler to go round, and only so many years he can keep winning bicycle races. So Ferdy came down from his mountain retreat in January and travelled with a number of Italians including Bartali and Bevilacqua to South America.

European cycling had nurtured a fascination with South America for several years already. Hugo Koblet was sniffing around Nicaragua and had only just returned from Central America where, according to reports, he had a whale of a time and might need a few weeks to recover. This time, Ferdy and his commission of eager promotional cyclists were touring the velodromes of Uruguay and Argentina in between photo opportunities with Eva Peron and the like. News hasn't escaped these lands that Ferdy Kübler is Champion of the World, yes the whole world, and those rainbow bands can't be kept locked up all winter.

If the intention was to spread the gospel of cycling, the holy water had been imbibed wholeheartedly and the natives were converting thanks to these missionaries from their civilised lands. Ferdy enjoyed the Argentine tango in particular while Gino Bartali smoked and drank his way through the early hours of the mornings before preaching his two-wheeled sermon on the velodromes of Buenos Aires and Montevideo. Nobody could keep up with him in either discipline.

For Ferdy, it was hardly the winter that Fritz Dietsche had always recommended for him when he joined the Tebag team – a winter of fresh mountain air and repose, away from velodromes, away from two wheels. It was a winter in preparation for a spring. He announced his intentions to ride Rome-Naples-Rome as well as Milano-Torino, to the surprise of the Italian authorities since he had been subjected to legal issues with the Fréjus team and had also run into trouble during last autumn's Lombardia race as well. He would go on to ride the Giro, too, because why not. If you're going to do one, you might as well do them all.

He won both the Tour du lac Léman as well as the Giro di Ticino. The knee was flaring up with alarming regularity, though. He pulled out of the Six Days of Paris and then withdrew in the first stage of Paris-Cote d'Azur with knee problems once more and questions were rightly being asked about Ferdy's calendar and whether, perhaps, he was due a rest. He'd take a few days off before riding a criterium against Hugo and Rome-Naples-Rome where he finished 7th.

Most importantly, he wanted to ride in Belgium. If not Flanders, then the Ardennes hills where last year he had won both Flèche-Wallonne and Liège-Bastogne-Liège in the same weekend. The fact that both races were now part of the Challenge Desgrange-Colombo, a sort of general classification across the whole road season, meant that the Ardennes Classics were top of everyone's list. The Belgians had been mopping up the Classics. Decoq had won Flanders, Schotte had taken Paris-Bruxelles and van Steenbergen had won Paris-Roubaix – but the Ardennes classics were of a very different nature – the climbs were longer and less punchy, and that would mean a different kind of Belgian would be a threat – namely Constantine Ockers or Raymond Impanis.

The Flèche-Wallonne would start on the Saturday morning under grey skies and cooler temperatures, leaving Loverval for Liège. There were multiple attempts at a breakaway which Ferdy and the other main contenders would work hard to retain within the group, and it wasn't until nearly 100km into the race that a small group got away with one Belgian and two French riders of little repute. They were kept within sight, but when their lead extended over the Côte de My, riders started breaking from the main group to join them – including Fritz Schär.

The breakaway had achieved a minute's gap on the main group, which was starting to cause friction. Ferdy thought that enough was enough, and Jean Robic felt the same. The two exploded away from the group in pursuit, leaving other riders look at one another – do we go? Do we stay? Ockers and Impanis reacted late and followed Ferdy and Robic whose pursuit had hit speeds of over 50km per hour.

Jean Robic punctured, leaving Ferdy to do the chasing, and when he joined the group just outside Liège, it was with Ockers and Impanis as well as the Frenchman Varnajo who was pulling hard at the front, looking to avoid a sprint at all costs. The Belgian Keteleer didn't fancy it either, and he pushed on the Côte de Theux outside town before attacking on the climbs in town as well, looking to distance Ferdy and Stan Ockers. The minor riders kept trying, but their only achievement was to drag Ferdy and Ockers to the line – Ferdy winning by a bike length from the Belgian.

The trouble with holding Liège-Bastogne-Liège the following day after a race as strenuous as the Flèche is that riders tend to take it easy until they have rounded Bastogne itself. Ten riders had got away just 10km into the race, but nobody took them seriously until around 40km from the end when Ferdy, Jean Robic – again, and a Belgian called Van Kerkhove formed a locomotive that would hunt down the breakaway in a handful of kilometres, disposing of them with disdain as it charged headlong into Liège. They would form the top three, and the least interesting aspect of what happened next was not that Ferdy Kubler won the sprint, but that Jean Robic would dismount his bicycle at the finish line and give Van Kerkhove a pretty serious right hook.

"You traitor!", screamed the man everyone knew as *Le Biquet* (the kid), planting a solid punch on the Belgian's ear.

"I was meant to win that bloody race! Ferdy and I had an agreement. That's all your fault."

Van Kerkhove responded in kind, pushing the little Breton back on his rear end before storming off to the safety of his team director.

Robic's issue with Van Kerkhove – as opposed to Ferdy with whom he supposedly had an agreement – was that the Belgian had sat on his wheel for the best part of 20km, refusing to take turns and, frankly, showing hardly enough respect for a man clearly his superior. When Van Kerkhove attacked in the final straight, Robic's resources had been drained, and only Ferdy could beat the Belgian at this point.

Did Ferdy actually agree that Jean Robic could win Liège? Turn this question on its head – would Ferdy Kübler have agreed to let someone else win the race when he had the opportunity to win the Double Double? Both Ardennes Classics in two successive years? For all of Ferdy's machinations, it seems highly unlikely that he would have simply said to Le Biquet – you know what, you can have this one.

If Ferdy had stayed out of the fisticuffs at the end of Liège, it only took one stage of the Giro d'Italia for Fiorenzo Magni to walk over and punch Ferdy clean in the face. It was a first stage that saw Hugo Koblet drop out of contention almost immediately with a puncture from which he couldn't recover, and the final sprint involved a large number of riders jockeying for position as they entered Bologna. According to Magni, Ferdy was holding onto his jersey – dangerous enough behaviour, but according to Ferdy, Magni was pushing him into the barriers. The two men had to be restrained as the commissioners gathered the evidence. The result would be a 2,000 lira fine for Ferdy, and a 5,000 lira fine for Magni – and Ferdy would be relegated to 18th place on the stage with the same time as the winner.

The two men kissed and made up the next morning in front of 10,000 people at the start line and the Giro settled into a standard format of breakaways and sprints for the next few days, the only notable exception to the rule being Hugo Koblet's evident lack of form. The Giro made its way to Rome after the tragic death of a young Italian rider, Orfeo Ponsin. Ferdy stood at the side of both Gino and Fausto at a mass held for the young rider, held by Pope Pius XII and later joined the Pope in conversation in German while the Pope later held conversations in English with the Australian riders, in French with Géminiani and Italian, of course, with the Italians.

In Roccacorso, the race organisers agreed to shorten the race by 30km due to the inclement weather, and even lit a fire at the start line so that the riders could dry themselves off. Fausto and team stayed in their cars while Ferdy rode around in a rain jacket wondering what on earth the problem was and why couldn't they just get on with the race.

And so, as the Giro wound its way back around Italy and up into the Dolomites, it started to take a more familiar aspect. The weather improved, and with it, so did Fausto Coppi. At the foot of the Dolomites, you could have considered the race wide open, but when a group of 10 men collided on the roads into Venice, Fausto saw his opportunity and signalled his intentions, riding into town and collecting the *maglia rosa*. The next day, Fausto flew over the Falazarego, the Pordoi and the Selle climbs to end the competition once and for all, leaving Ferdy six minutes back in fourth place on the stage, unable to respond to the effervescent Italian.

And really, when this happens, a Grand Tour begins its long coda, the only question being who would follow up behind Coppi in 2nd and 3rd place. Magni and Kübler, those combatants from the first stage, would sprint it out, but Magni's advantage remained right up to the final stage, and Ferdy would content himself with third place and the green jersey for the best-placed foreigner in the race. Ferdy had obtained a podium place, but contractual wrangles with the Fréjus company who had backed him left a sour taste. They accused him of racing the Baracchi Trophy on a Swiss bicycle, and not the Italian bicycle he was contractually committed to racing, and had furthermore discovered that Ferdy had been racing on his Swiss bicycle even in Belgium. The Italian company listed the races and, handily, the amount he had won for each race, and tried to claim over 5,600,000 lira from Ferdy, a still painful but more manageable 40,000 Swiss francs.

The wrangling would continue throughout the summer, but had nothing to do with Ferdy's decision not to ride the Tour de France which was almost entirely due to tiredness brought on by not stopping since January.

You could argue that the Tour de Suisse, which took place mid-June in between the two Grand Tours, was always going to be a struggle for Ferdy, what with the knee, the tiredness and the legal problems in the background playing on his mind, but the topic of conversation had since moved on. Instead, all anyone could talk about was how Hugo Koblet was unwell, and all Ferdy could think about was how Hugo Koblet was sweating, was so far behind that it didn't feel right, was not the man he knew. We might be rivals, thought Ferdy, but we're still human beings, his mother still needs reassuring, we still need each other.

The controversial end to Hugo's Tour de Suisse masked Ferdy's dip in form, but gave Rösli every reason to call her man home for the summer. You've done enough, Ferdinand. You've done enough. Now rest.

1953

LOST
AND
FOUND

It was that liminal time of year. Is it late spring, or is it early summer? The Eglis had withdrawn from the city many years ago and watched the changes of seasons marked not by road races or Grand Tours, but by the growth of plants on their smallholding in Dürnten, by the list of tasks that changed each day – pruning the roses, clearing the leaves, shovelling the snow, planting the tomato seeds over the fireplace...

Paul Egli had, and his wife would use the word 'mercifully', calmed down somewhat since his cycling years. He had probably always been seeking the quiet life, without ever really knowing how to get there. And now here he is, his bicycle packed neatly away in the garage, used perhaps on Sundays, if the weather is fair. He had withdrawn almost wholly from cycling, although journalists would still call every other day, seeking his opinion on all things with two wheels. What was, for instance, his opinion on the declining form of Ferdy Kübler, the misadventures of Hugo Koblet, the state of Swiss cycling in general? Occasionally, someone like Walter Grimm would pitch up at the front door, all cheery smiles, with a packet of seeds and, Paul couldn't help but notice, a notebook.

It wasn't Walter Grimm at the door that morning. It was, as forewarned, the now 34-year-old Ferdinand Kübler who stood at the farmhouse door, his hair a little shorter than before, his face a little more drawn. I know that look, he thought. I *was* that look. The two embraced and Ferdy was welcomed inside, offered a drink.

Paul and Ferdy had maintained a strong teacher-pupil dynamic. Silvia Egli knew that when Ferdy turns up, it's time to leave the men to their lessons. She withdraws to the herb garden. This time, it looks serious.

Ferdy was depressed. Not clinically, more in a self-obsessed-sulky kind of way. 1953 had been a poor vintage thus far. There would be no triple double in the Ardennes weekend, even though technically, you could say that he won the weekend by finishing 2nd in Flèche Wallonne and 7th in Liège-Bastogne-Liège. Nobody really considers that a victory though. Rome–Naples–Rome followed and it wasn't very good. Worse, Hugo came fourth that day, and Hugo looked good.

Even worse, Ferdy entered the Tour de Romandie hoping to arrest the downturn, only to find Hugo ahead of him on the first stage and then taking ridiculous risks on the descent of the Saint-Cergues in the second stage. Ferdy came home several minutes later and wondered what on earth he had to do. Not to worry, he thought, there's a time trial tomorrow. And yet Hugo's time trialling had never really suffered. Ferdy lost over four minutes on him, but then again, so did Louison. Ferdy did win the last two stages, but only because Hugo let him, or maybe Hugo didn't care because he'd already won the Tour de Romandie and Ferdy hadn't.

He was then invited to join the Guerra team for the Giro d'Italia, because who doesn't want a fighter like Ferdy Kübler. Or, as Ferdy understood it, he took the invitation because it was the only one he received and he didn't want to miss out on everything. The humiliation though, of having to support Hugo Koblet and little Fritzi Schär, and then withdrawing after just one stage. The humiliation of the excoriating press the next day, the humiliation of having to listen to the not-so-quiet whispers from the other riders that not only is Ferdy on the decline, but Ferdy couldn't be bothered. Couldn't bring himself to help his great rival, and after all – why would he? This is Ferdy and all Ferdy is interested in is Ferdy.

He's yesterday's man. Finally. Not so much whispers as a lot of people shouting very loudly.

Abandoning the Giro was not an act of humiliation, it was the result of humiliation. From the moment Ferdy accepted the invitation to ride, he was looking for a way out.

Decline was inevitable. Decline had to be managed, but did decline have to hurt so much? It came at that precise moment that Hugo had returned to form, that Fausto was riding like a man possessed. Ferdy looked at the peloton and looked at the bloodshot eyes and the sweat, and saw riders who peaked one day, fell back the next. While Ferdy was getting older on mineral water and orange juice, others were high on amphetamines, distancing him with alarming regularity. Hugo and Fausto were openly doping while Ferdy slept 9 hours a day, living like a monk.

"All anyone talks about is Hugo," moaned Ferdy, slumped in Paul Egli's favourite armchair.

"He didn't even win the bloody Giro but they welcomed him home as if he'd trounced Fausto. Nobody even remembers my name anymore."

Egli recognised the symptoms. He and Paul Amberg had nurtured a profitable dislike for each other over the years. It started off as a bargain of sorts – you hate me, I'll hate you and together we'll own the press. Rivalries can be manufactured to further careers, enhance your profile, and then over time they grow legs, start to live on their own terms. Within time, he genuinely despised Amberg, without really knowing why.

Ferdy and Hugo was different. It was a rivalry principally driven by Ferdy's refusal to give in to decline. Egli and Amberg were of the same age, but Ferdy and Hugo were six years apart. Ferdy had been riding for over seven years before Hugo started racing, ten before the Giro of 1950, and what had he won until then? Nothing. Well, nothing of note. It took the handsome young Hugo to shake Ferdy to his senses. Egli wished that Hugo had come along sooner, it might have helped.

The tail-end of a career can be bruising, he reflected. You have been overtaken by younger, fitter men. Your bicycle no longer accelerates at the same pace, and yet you feel young, you feel that the legs of yesteryear are only a revolution away. Sunsets take so long to dip below the horizon.

A rider can go in any of several directions. Firstly, he can refuse to accept his decline, carry on racing and humiliating himself until he becomes a joke. Secondly, he can line up a second career as the wise old head of the peloton. Louis Caput is doing that already, marshalling riders and giving orders. He will doubtless go on to become a technical director, bellowing instructions from the passenger door of a team car. Or thirdly, he can pick off a few winnable races and bow out on a high.

Paul Egli liked the latter option. It seemed more Ferdy Kübler than the other two, although at this rate, Ferdy was heading for the first option.

The tail-end of his own career could have been better managed. He often wishes that he had tried again for a Tour de Suisse, but instead he focused on moulding Ferdy, making a man out of him. And when Ferdy became that man, Paul saw the fruit of his efforts flying off up the mountain ahead of him while he struggled gamely to keep up. And so Paul Egli put his bike away, broke the team up and tried to cut all ties to the sport. If only I'd done it differently, he thought to himself. If only I'd gone for one big effort.

"Why don't you try Bordeaux-Paris," he mused,

almost surprising himself at the suggestion.

Ferdy was silent. He shuffled in his armchair. Bordeaux-Paris. He rolled the names of the two cities around his mouth as if trying them out for size. Bordeaux-Paris. It's the hardest race of them all. Over 500km. Bordeaux-Paris…

"It's been put back this year, so you'll have time to train for it."

Ferdy sat up straight, thinking of the headlines. He'd do it. He knew he'd do it. He just had to find a way of articulating that he would do it. It would require weeks of training. It would require a whole team around him, someone to ride the derny, someone to prepare the food, someone to drive the car… but through the cloud of logistics and the haze of how-to's and how-not-to's, Ferdy knew that he would do it.

And he knew that Hugo wouldn't do it.

Hugo, meanwhile, had found his legs. He had spent most of last year looking for them. It turned out they were at the Velodrome d'Hiver in Paris, in the cold of January.

Together with Armin von Buren, Hugo took on the omnium specialists Emile Carrara and Georges Senfftleben and defeated them in a deciding round. He lost the sprint to Emile, but he could feel the legs returning, the pedals turning with greater ease than at any point in 1952.

Armin and Hugo travelled back home to Zürich where they became European Champions in the Six Days, and Hugo felt better than ever. He still carried a few pounds from winter, but he was shedding them with every revolution of every velodrome that would have him. So he put his name forward for Milan-San Remo. He felt at home in Italy.

Hugo attacked from the start, taking French rider Georges Decaux with him for a 200km-long breakaway that lasted until the slopes of the Turchino before discovering that the peloton had found them. It wasn't a winning move; the peloton housed him for a short while before he waved goodbye to them and rode into San Remo alone, but the signs were good. He could still ride a bike and with a few more races under his belt, he would be winning Tours with the simplicity and audacity of '50 and '51.

Ferdy was still plugging away like an annoying fly, though. They met in the Tour de Romandie and Hugo saw him off in a sprint in the first stage. The next day, Ferdy flew off up the mountain while Hugo struggled with his breathing, so he took the descent as if his whole career depended on it. Team cars struggled to keep up with a rampant Hugo who tore the mountain to pieces, retrieving the deficit and most importantly, not letting Ferdy get away. He needn't have worried, as he won the time trial comfortably the next day, waiting with his stopwatch to see exactly when Ferdy would arrive. It didn't matter that Ferdy won the last two stages of the race, it just mattered that Hugo had returned.

But that climb in the second stage up Saint-Cergues was a worry. It was only 1,500m, the only real challenge of this edition of Romandie, and yet it led to Hugo taking all manner of risks in order to re-establish his margin on the descent. As the climb took hold, all Hugo could think about was the look on Dr Rupf's face as he explained to Hugo why a deficiency of red blood cells would make climbing more difficult.

Hugo would put it down to preparation. The Giro was the plan all along, of course. It had been just three years since Hugo announced himself to the world, and now he could return as one of the favourites. His good friend Fausto Coppi was the clear favourite, but now Louison Bobet had grown in maturity. His first Grand Tour win would surely come soon; he would be a danger.

And yet Hugo could not have known that he, himself, would be the danger to everyone else. Over the first few stages of the Giro, Hugo attacked and tormented the peloton with regularity, looking for – and failing to hold – an advantage. Senior voices such as Raphaël Géminiani wondered openly why they had to ride at 50km per hour. Why didn't Hugo slow things down? After all, as one of the leaders of the peloton, he had earned that right.

The fourth stage was no exception. Hugo attacked relentlessly, forcing Géminiani and his French teammates to bring him back, call him to reason. Coppi, Bartali, Bobet and van Steenbergen all put in shifts to haul Hugo back into their midst, and teams began to voice the idea that eliminating Hugo, one way or another, would be to everyone's advantage. Not because Hugo would necessarily win the Giro, but because he's riding a three-week race like it's a one-day Classic.

A flashpoint was always likely to happen. It would come at the feed station near Popoli. A group of 50 riders had called for calm, slowing down in advance so that all could eat in peace. Since feed stations were no longer neutralised, these were gentleman's agreements and could just as easily be broken. It was an Italian, Vittorio Rossello, who broke the agreement and raced into Popoli ahead of the peloton. Hugo instinctively followed, breaking from the group to chase down the ambitious little Italian.

The route through Popoli took in a number of right angles, 90-degree turns beyond which you couldn't see past the heads of the packed crowds. It was lively and loud, no place to chase a young rider over 30 minutes down on the general classification.

Rossello emptied his musette and cast it to the side, but it caught on his handlebars and landed in the road. There were no barriers, so the *tifosi* descended upon it. A small girl broke free and ran towards the musette, unaware that there was a rider approaching, head down, at 50km per hour.

Witnesses recalled that Koblet somersaulted over his bicycle. Some said that he was launched three metres into the air, falling with an enormous thump onto the side of the road. He flew so high that people had time to get out of the way, create space for him to land. The child lay motionless on the ground like a broken doll. Blood ran through the cobblestones. There was silence for an eternal split second, and then screams.

Jean Bobet found himself alongside Coppi, van Steenbergen and Bartali, riding past the awful scene. They called Louison and Raphaël Géminiani over. We need to work together. Catch Rossello.

It took five kilometres of hard racing to reel him in, but Rossello knew nothing of the incident behind. He leapt away again, and it took Fausto Coppi to sprint after him, practically wrestling his bicycle to a standstill. The orders went out, first from Fausto, secondly from Louison for the benefit of those who could not speak Italian – no one attacks. No one rides. *Personne n'attaque*. The race would be neutralised.

Stragglers joined the peloton with updates. Hugo wasn't moving. Hugo is dead. He killed a girl and killed himself. The peloton rode, dumbstruck, as one at a funereal 30km/h with Coppi and Bobet ensuring nobody could break from the front. If Hugo really were dead, who would want to win such a stage.

Journalists came next, leaning out of car windows. Hugo is conscious. Hugo is back on his bike. The girl is breathing. All is well.

With his five Swiss teammates, Hugo was making time on the idling peloton, and in time he would reintegrate that peloton, a peloton that had started the day cursing him for making them ride so hard but would end it relieved that he was still alive. Hugo knew that even though Fausto had won the sprint in Roccaroso, the whole stage had been about him. He had taunted his fellow riders, attacked needlessly and nearly killed a child. His teammates had waited for him, racked with worry as he was pulled from the pavement. They had put him back on his bike and paced him back into the race, and then he rode so hard he left them behind, only to realise they had neutralised the whole Giro d'Italia just for him.

It was one thing to return to form, quite another to return to the fold.

Hugo took it easy for the next few stages, waiting for the time trial between Grossetto and Follonica, a distance of just 48km. He won so convincingly that he took the maglia rosa from Giuseppe Minardo and finished 1'21" ahead of Fausto and over three minutes ahead of the supposedly promising Louison. There would be a team trial a few days later, which would surely be a stiffer task. The Swiss team was down to just four men after the Kübleriste withdrawals of Ferdy, Croci-Torti and Graf, leaving Hugo with just Fritz Schär, Walter Diggelmann and Remo Pianezzi.

Against all odds though, the Swiss team lost only 26 seconds to Coppi's Bianchi outfit and Hugo kept the *maglia rosa* and even managed to add a further minute to his lead over Fausto between Vicenza and Auronzo, attacking once more on the descent.

Time was running out for the other general classification contenders. The Giro would be Hugo's if he could survive the final two stages. Firstly,

Auronzo to Bolzano, a stage that would start with a 24km climb up to the Misurina Lake. As the temperature dropped, the roads narrowed and Primo Volpi took the initiative and broke from the leading group. Hugo followed with Coppi, Bobet and Ockers in hot pursuit. The quartet bridged to Volpi and left him behind with the Pordoi still to come.

The Pordoi can be a frightening prospect at the best of times. When Hugo started the climb, a blanket of frozen fog had descended over the mountain, restricting his breathing. He climbed nonetheless. At the summit, 2,239m high, he took a newspaper, shoved it down his jersey to hold off the cold of the 7km descent while cries of *Venga Coppi, Venga Coppi* rang down the mountainside. Coppi was on his way, dancing on his pedals and eating into Hugo's advantage. By the time Hugo reached the Colle della Sella, Coppi could see his target and in the space of two kilometres, he had caught him, gone past and distanced him. Even Pasquale Fornara flew past. If Hugo were to keep his *maglia rosa*, it would come down to the descent.

Hugo attacked every corner with Coppi in his line of sight. Fornara was caught and left behind complaining about his brakes not working, not taking any risks. Hugo took them all for him as he joined Coppi just three kilometres from the finish.

"How many minutes have we got on them?" asked Hugo.

"Enough for us to ride into Bolzano together," smiled Fausto. And then, patting Hugo on the back, he added "Congratulations! You've won the Giro!"

Fausto was allowed to win the stage. For Hugo, the Giro.

Did Hugo take this as a pact? A concession? Certainly, Fausto Coppi appeared not to believe he would win the Giro, and he may well have believed – when riding into Bolzano – that the race was indeed Hugo's. Even if Coppi were to attack on the Stelvio the next day, it would take a superhuman effort.

So when the Bianchi team sat down for dinner that evening, the conversation should have been about a podium place, and perhaps that was what Fausto Coppi was expecting. Ettore Milano, the Bianchi team boss, had other ideas.

"Tomorrow, we're riding the highest point of this Tour, over 3,000m of altitude. We all know that Hugo Koblet weakens when he reaches 1,500m. You know it Fausto, we have to try."

Publicly, the message from Bianchi was that Hugo Koblet had won the Tour, that there would be no attack on the Stelvio, and that Fausto was happy with his place on the podium. As a result, some journalists packed their bags and went home. The race was as good as over.

Fausto Coppi went to bed, content with second place. Ettore Milano awoke, alive to the possibilities.

It was Ettore Milano who first noticed Hugo Koblet's condition that morning. He's wearing sunglasses, he whispered to anyone who would hear him. I need to see his eyes. He's sweating, he would tell others. I need to get a closer look.

His ruse was to ask a photographer to get a shot of Koblet, convince him to take the sunglasses off. Hugo acquiesced and Milano knew that Coppi would win the Giro the precise split second that he saw Hugo's bloodshot eyes.

Had Hugo been taking amphetamines since the start of the Giro? Quite possibly, but probably not. It is, however, entirely possible that the previous day had taken its toll on Hugo, and that the only way to get through the Queen stage of the race was to dope. Milano ran over to his rider – Fausto, Fausto, you'll never believe what I've just seen. Hugo has been doping – his eyes are bloodshot, he's sweating like a horse. I swear, Fausto, you're going to win the Giro!

Fausto took his sunglasses off in turn and revealed similarly bloodshot eyes. Ettore, he replied, I've been taking *la bomba* as well. We're all in the same boat.

What Hugo had been suffering from was not *la bomba* – which would eventually ensure he could at least climb the first few kilometres of the Stelvio climb. He was suffering from insomnia, a side-effect of too many amphetamines. Another side-effect was thirst. Over the first few kilometres of this penultimate stage of the Giro d'Italia, Ettore Milano kept a close eye on Hugo, reporting back to all who would hear him – he's gone through another bidon. He's cooked, I tell you, Hugo's cooked! Fausto Coppi turned back to the team car and laconically replied, "well so am I", before downing another bidon himself.

This phoney war didn't last long. After 80km of the stage, at the foot of the Stelvio, Coppi could be seen talking to one of his gregarii, Andréa Carrea. Papagallo, he shouted, why are you going so hard? Carrea understood the coded message, and he leapt from the front of the group. His attack stretched the leading group and soon only five men were left – Koblet, Coppi, Bartali, Fornara and a young rider called Nino Defilippis.

Coppi rode alongside Defilippis and asked him to attack next. The youngster shook his head – Mr Coppi, sir, I can't. I'm on my limit. But Coppi insisted. It will be good for your career, for your future as a professional bike racer, if you could help me out now. So with what little Nino Defilippis had left in the tank, he did as he was told. What possessed Hugo Koblet to follow, no one will know. He didn't need to respond to Defilippis' attack, but instinct told him to go. As Hugo used up his reserves bridging across, Fausto Coppi shot past like a motorbike, shattering the pact they had made the previous day.

At first, Hugo was floored by the move. Yesterday they were friends, patting each other on the back and celebrating Hugo's win together. Today, Fausto has stabbed him in the back, and now he's twisting the knife. In next to no time, Fausto was so far ahead of Hugo that he was out of sight.

Hugo gritted his teeth as it dawned on him that the race was not yet lost. As the air thinned, Hugo's breathing became more restricted and Hugo withdrew into his own personal oblivion. Learco

Guerra could have been singing the Swiss national anthem from the window of his car for all Hugo knew, he would never have heard. Sunlit banks of snow were blinding him. The Stelvio, never before climbed in the Giro d'Italia, had claimed its first victim.

Coppi crested the summit of the Stelvio, acknowledging a lady in a white coat as he did so. The assembled crowds at the peak waited for the maglia rosa, but first came Fornara, over two minutes behind Coppi. Bartali came 30 seconds later to rapturous applause. Andréa Carrea, the man who had started it all, came in just over a minute later, and 4'27" down on Coppi came Hugo Koblet, the *maglia rosa* for now, but unless he could master the descent into Bormio, no longer the leader of the Giro d'Italia.

Hugo took all the risks he could, entering each corner with greater speed than is safe. Twice he fell on the descent, once he punctured, but he kept racing, kept riding as fast as he knew how. He picked up a whole minute on the descent down the Stelvio but on his arrival into Bormio, it was clear that the Giro was gone.

Just one hour later, Hugo and Fausto crossed each other in the hotel corridor. Wracked with shame, Fausto's first thought was to thank Hugo, but that felt wrong. To apologise, perhaps, to say something, anything that would excuse the broken pact, if it were a pact, if there really were an agreement. Hugo glared at his rival in silence and returned to his room.

Fausto would have been happy with second place but couldn't resist the urgings of his teammates and colleagues. The result was a bittersweet Giro victory, the reality was that he had lost a friend.

An angry Hugo returned to Switzerland where he won the Tour de Suisse in vengeful fashion, dominating the race from the second day and even winning the final stage back into Zürich by an embarrassing 12 minutes and 20 seconds over the rider in 2nd place. It was a demonstration, a demolition that Ferdy Kübler did well to avoid, sat at home with his baby daughter.

It was confirmation, for many, that Hugo was back. Last year was a blip.

STUDEBAKER

You don't see many Studebakers in Strasbourg. Citroëns, yes. Renaults too. German cars are welcome here. But Studebakers are long and sleek, and – hide your envy – American. So it could only be one man in that Studebaker, *le Bel Hugo*, the Apollo-on-a-bike that thousands upon thousands of Strasburgers had gathered to glimpse, Hugo Koblet.

The Studebaker circled the Town Hall before parking, illegally, in front of it. Everything is permitted where Hugo Koblet is concerned – you can park wherever you want, you can even drive American cars and get away with it. The driver-side door opened first, revealing first the reflective blonde hair of the Swiss cyclist, his excessive suntan, his tailored shirt with two buttons on each cuff. How elegant, how James Dean.

Hugo moved, no - he glided around the car, opening the rear passenger door to reveal the wife of his doctor, Eugen Rupf, followed shortly by Dr

Rupf himself. And then, with such grace, he strolled around to the front passenger door and opened it to reveal the plus-sized frame of his brother Adolf. Adolf was not accustomed to adoring crowds, turning to them to yell at the top of his voice, "we've had a lovely journey", before being ushered to somewhere he could not be heard.

This display at an end, journalists made their move, thrusting microphones under Hugo's perfect nose. Speak, say something, please.

"What a shame Fausto Coppi couldn't be here," he started while taking autograph books from approaching girls and signing them copiously. "It'll now be down to me to manage the race and mark my rivals. I don't think Gino Bartali will try anything on the flat stages and everyone will be watching me because of what I did between Brive and Agen. But without Coppi, will any victory be as sweet?"

A journalist: "What do you fear Hugo?"

"Fear? Well, Bobet has already raced the Tour six times. He has the experience. Then there's Bartali and Robic, they're always present. And if you'll excuse me," he motioned towards the hotel, "I'm going to take a bath."

Of course he is, they all acquiesced. How very Hugo.

Hugo let Dr Rupf inform the remaining journalists of his health and he did exactly as he had promised. He took a bath.

Stage one followed a well-trodden Tour de France route, from Strasbourg to Metz. A relatively serene

Hugo Koblet controlled the peloton which housed the contenders for the general classification, leaving his compatriot Fritz Schär to rule the breakaway and eventually to take the yellow jersey with a full 12 minutes' advantage over the field. Did Hugo mind? Not at all, in fact it added to the atmosphere within the Swiss camp, and Schär always falls apart at the first sniff of mountain air.

Schär won stage two as well, but the Swiss team was being whittled down day-by-day. Ferdy Kübler's best friend, and therefore the disloyal Emilio Croci-Torti had departed after just one stage. A Kübleresque gesture, perhaps orchestrated from afar by Hugo's rival? Even for Hugo, this was far-fetched but not dismissed by some journalists. Two other riders, Chevalley and Meili, missed the cut, arriving at the finish line far too late to be allowed to race stage three.

A peloton always looks for a *chef*, someone to tell riders what to do, who can go ahead, to dictate the pace. This year, without Coppi, the responsibility fell to Hugo. But Hugo's instincts were not those of a *chef du peloton*. He thought back to '51 and how he won the Tour before the Italians could start their climbs, he thought of Saint-Cergues and how he was forced to make time up on the descents. And so Hugo attacked repeatedly. He attacked at feeding stations, stretching the peloton out at points where they least expected it. He would chase down breakaways at breakneck speeds of 50km per hour. At the start of every stage, he would make a list of the top twenty riders in the general classification, fold it up and put it in his back pocket alongside his comb. When a breakaway formed, Hugo would withdraw the piece of paper, unfold it and study the names. Who has gone, he would ask. Names would be shouted out and if they were on the list, they would be chased down. If not, they were allowed to ride. When a breakaway was allowed to form, it was either chased down or left to its own devices, and if it were the latter, then Hugo would ensure he won every peloton sprint going. In Dieppe, he won the sprint for 7th, and the next day he won the sprint for 9th place. In Le Mans, he won the sprint for 10th, the next day beating young sprinter André Darrigade and others for 8th.

Why, asked the other riders, is the *chef du peloton* trying to out-sprint us all for minor places?

Surely, come the first mountain stage from Pau to Cautarets, Hugo would leave us all in peace? There would be the Aubisque, the Soulor and finally Cautarets itself.

A breakaway formed. Hugo retrieved the piece of paper from his back pocket and nodded as the names of Darrigade, Drei and Huber were called out. The trio were allowed a three-minute advantage at the foot of the Aubisque, until Hugo decided enough was enough and he raced up the Aubisque, leaving his principal competitors for dead. So much for Dr Rupf's warnings about red blood cells. Hugo was back and Hugo was dominating the Tour.

Or was he. Once Hugo reached the Soulor, he started to weaken. Bobet and Robic passed him with little apparent effort and the Swiss champion was forced to acknowledge that he had wasted his energy chasing down a breakaway that would have been caught sooner or later, regardless. Once more, the higher Hugo went, the worse he felt. Red blood cells. His chest tightened, his breathing became more laboured. He hauled his body and bicycle over the Aubisque and prepared for the descent à tombeau ouverte, an open-coffin descent as the French would call it. Riding often at speeds in excess of 80km per hour, Hugo took the same risks as he took in Romandie and at the Giro, spitting stones from the road, watching his wheel vibrate on loose gravel. He overtook rider after rider, Marcel Huber included, before a wheel stuck, twisted too far. The handlebars shook to the side, Hugo left the road, detached from his machine.

How many times did he land? Two, three times? The first was the hardest, the explosion of dust marking his point of impact. The second was front-on, the third hurt the most.

And then silence fell. A ringing in the ears followed by the sounds of bicycles passing, the squeals of brakes, shouts in the distance, and then nothing again. Just Hugo and the mountain.

One by one, they went to search for Hugo. Marcel Huber was one of the first on the scene. He's over here, in the heather. Alex Burtin was next. Felix Lévitan, Tour organiser, was there next. André

Leducq, hero of Tours gone by and now walking mouthpiece, jumped out of Lévitan's car. Hugo wasn't moving. Best not to move him, someone said, we don't know what's broken. An ambulance was on its way. The race neutralised. Someone tell his mother.

It could have been so much worse. In the end, the diagnosis was multiple broken ribs, cuts, bruises, torn ligaments and ultimately, the worst diagnosis of all, a withdrawal from the Tour. Of course. Not even the great Hugo Koblet could get up from this. They swaddled Hugo in blankets, lay him in the back of the car and drove as quickly as the car would allow them. Forget the ambulance, it's taking too long.

For once, though, this wasn't a case of a rider saying goodbye to the Tour de France, it was the Tour saying goodbye to a rider. Lévitan waxed lyrical in his daily column about the purest, most beautiful Hugo, without whom this Tour would be less pure and less beautiful. The Italian team mechanic later found his way into Hugo's hotel room to leave a present on his bedside table, "because I admire you so much, Hugo."

Riders who had been run ragged by Hugo came, one by one, echoing these sentiments, leaving flowers, cards and wishes. It was a drawn-out and sincere goodbye from men who saw in Hugo a little of themselves. Admittedly, they had little of Hugo's good looks, and in most cases, little of his fortune, but they all knew that at any moment, they could suffer the same fate. So they came, said their sad goodbyes, got on their bikes and left Hugo behind, along with the rest of the Tour, its *caravane*, its press pack and its hangers-on, and the show left town.

PACTS AND CONTRACTS

Shortly after Fausto Coppi had broken his pact with Hugo, he was on the lookout for new agreements. It was mid-August, the heat was breaking. Fausto and Ferdy had sat out the Tour de France, a decision neither would particularly rue, for different reasons. They had finished the Prix des As in front of 14,000 spectators in the Valais canton of Switzerland. A parochial affair, a bit of fun, a chance to catch up with friends. And good money.

They sat together at a table for two, Ferdy treating Fausto to some of the local Valaisienne cuisine.

Fausto pushed his food around, a man with something to ask, searching for a way to ask it.

"Ferdinando", he started. "I've never won the World Championships. If you and I race against each other, neither of us will win."

Ferdy thought about this. The rainbow jersey had probably been the last thing on his mind, he was more interested in Bordeaux-Paris.

Fausto persisted. "Think about it Ferdinando. We are the same age, you and I. You've been world champion, but could you help me become world champion too? What do you say? At the very least, we could agree on a pact of, how do you say, non-aggression?"

Ferdy had always seen the World Championships as a one-off. Win it once, and you've won it forever. What's more, last year's race was a disaster for the sport. Nobody knew who Heinz Muller was then, and nobody knows now. If anything, his win devalues the race itself. No, the World Championship should go to the best rider in the sport once in his career, and everyone will benefit if Fausto wins it.

"It's a deal," smiled Ferdy. "Non-aggression. If one of us escapes, the other manages the chase. And in that case, I'll do everything I can to help you."

Fausto raised a glass, went to bed early and woke early to continue his meticulous training regime. It is unlikely that he had not formed agreements with other riders. Just like Ferdy, Fausto was looking over his shoulder at younger, sometimes faster opponents. It doesn't matter how much *la bomba* you took, it was just getting harder. If enough men could be convinced that a Fausto win would be to their benefit as well as Fausto's, then the Worlds would be his, finally.

Did Fausto see Ferdy as a threat to his rainbow bands? It was only two years ago that Ferdy took an entire summer off to prepare for the Worlds in Varese, and now here's Ferdy, taking the summer off to prepare for what exactly?

Two thirds into the World Road Race in Lugano, Fausto did exactly what he had told Ferdy he would do – he attacked. The Belgian Germain Derycke went with him in the vain hope that he might compete, or more realistically compete for silver. Behind, a chase group organised which included Louison Bobet and... Ferdy Kübler. Who else.

Men took turns on the front until Louison flicked his elbow at Ferdy, who remained passive within the group, head down. Bobet flicked his elbow again. Do your turn. Come on.

Still nothing.

"What the fuck's going on Ferdy? Take your turn!"

And then, a look of realisation crept over Louison's face. "Ahhh. You're riding for Coppi aren't you! You total bastard."

In his best broken French, Ferdy pointed at his knee and said "I can't. Bad knee."

Coppi finished six minutes ahead, a distance so crushing that even on his best days of his best years, Ferdy would have struggled to bridge the gap, and who knows who else within that chase group had been given a promise by Fausto – you can win a different race, I'll give you this amount of money, here's a criterium invitation. Whatever you want, so long as I get to win my World Championships.

None of this mattered to Louison, who was obviously not part of any deal going; he gave Ferdy the silent treatment for a further two weeks before picking up the phone and asking him what the hell he was doing.

"I'm preparing for a rather big race, Louison," replied Ferdy. "You'll never believe it, but…"

Bordeaux-Paris is a stupid race. A relic. But it's also a great race, a legendary race, and if you really want your name to go down in history, you'll ride "the derby".

It is a race of antiquity. 560km long, half of it ridden behind a derny – one of those motorised bikes that allows riders to 'pace' behind them and maintain higher speeds for longer periods. Who rides ridiculous distances like this anymore? Bike racing is changing, it is becoming more athletic. There are more races to choose from than ever before, and yet Bordeaux-Paris still has an allure for certain riders, it pulls them in and makes fools or heroes of them.

Ferdy Kübler had made his mind up to race the 1953 edition because his season was falling apart in front of his eyes. Hugo Koblet's name was plastered all over the newspapers day-in, day-out. There were rumours of love affairs, and it barely mattered whether he won or lost on the road or the track, everyone wanted to hear about Hugo Koblet; Ferdy was a footnote.

And if Ferdy hated anything, it was being a footnote. But I'll show them all, he thought. I'll write my name in legend and it will be the name of Ferdy Kübler on the front pages of all the newspapers! You'd never find Hugo racing the derby!

Therefore, it was decided. Ferdy would ride this stupid, great race of antiquity. Team Director at "La Perle", Francis Pélissier agreed to train and equip him for the race. Under certain conditions. You must arrive several days in advance, he warned his rider. Our preparation will be meticulous, and you must sleep for long hours. Yes, yes, said Ferdy, half-remembering some velodrome contracts that he had signed. Remembering not to mention them to Pélissier.

When Pélissier discovered that Ferdy intended to race on the Thursday evening ahead of the race at the Oerlikon, he flew into a rage. I want fresh legs for this race! Fresh legs! And what do you give me? A man who races all night at a velodrome. Either you show up at my offices on Wednesday or you can consider our contract broken!

Well, thought Ferdy. It's not my fault they moved the date of Bordeaux-Paris, and besides, Hugo is racing that night as well. I can hardly let him keep all the headlines to himself. He would even team up with Hugo in a team pursuit, and they would beat Patterson and van Steenbergen, and this would be good for both of them. And then, as soon as the meeting ends, Ferdy would jump into the back of Rolf Graf's car, lie down on the back seat and sleep as Rolf drove them to Paris. He would catch the train, sleep some more on the train, and be in Bordeaux with a full night's sleep ahead of him. It has all been planned, just not how you would have planned it. All will be fine.

Francis Pélissier would have none of this, and telegrammed Ferdy to inform him that he would not support him. Undeterred, Ferdy called his old boss, Fritz Dietsche, who jumped at the chance to equip his former protégé.

His first task was to mummify Ferdy – an unusual preparation but one which all the participants of Bordeaux-Paris undertook ahead of the race on the advice of their *soigneurs*.

His second task would be to ensure that Ferdy would have enough food to last the race. Chickens, minced meat, rice cakes, sugared drinks, figs... everything was ordered from local butchers and delicatessens to provide Ferdy with the perfect nutritional balance for a race that would test him to his very limits.

This edition of Bordeaux-Paris would have only eight participants. There were twelve riders registered, but people always drop out once they realise once they've signed up to. The favourite would be Wim Van Est. He had already won it twice, in 1950 and 1952, and of course you had Stan Ockers who could ride all day and loved the derny. Ferdy was an unknown – untested over this distance and still with a reputation for going too hard, too soon.

The riders would leave Bordeaux at one in the morning in driving rain. Their bikes were not equipped with lights, so they had to follow the lights of the race vehicles ahead of them as their wheels slipped and skidded on the wet surface. It was a near-perfect replica of pre-war Tours where men fought against the elements in the dark, fighting against the urge to sleep.

There would be a break at eight in the morning, a chance to change into some dry clothing, and after 253 kilometres of riding, Fernand Wambst would be waiting on a derny bike along with seven other men on similar machines. Seeing their men approach, they slid goggles over their eyes, tweaked the peaks of their caps and set out on the road, allowing their riders to slip in behind and pick up the pace. The Breton Mahé felt good, felt like he had an attack in him, so he made a move as the race entered the vineyard and chateau-dotted fields of the Loire valley. Behind, Wim Van Est and Ferdy Kübler were forming a line of four behind their respective dernies, trying to bridge the gap. They discovered Mahé running out of gas 100km later at Orleans, but Ferdy punctured and saw the two men ride off into the distance.

Over the following 22km, Ferdy upped the pace to nearly 60km per hour behind Wambst, not even stopping to take food from the car behind. It was a magnificent effort from a man who had been racing since one in the morning with only a couple of short breaks over the last 500km.

"Go quicker" he screamed at Wambst.

Wambst shook his head. "Eat."

"Fuck the food. Get a move on!"

Wambst shook his head again. What was he doing? Why would Wambst not increase the pace? Van Est was beginning to struggle, one attack could floor him. But Fernand Wambst knew what he was doing. As Ferdy cursed behind him, Wambst refused to increase the pace and continued to insist that Ferdy eat. He had won this race himself, and what's more he had trained a Belgian rider, Poels, who had refused to eat. When Poels was leading at Versailles, he started to bonk – cycling lingo for that horrible moment the body runs out of energy. Wambst knew that he had a potential winner behind him, and he wasn't going to let it happen again.

And Wambst was right. Van Est was tiring, and by the time the riders had reached Versailles, Van Est was starting to struggle to hold onto his derny. In the Parc des Princes velodrome, Ferdy had already stretched away from the Dutchman whose derny was a good five seconds ahead of him, and won the derby with something to spare.

The result was precisely what Ferdy had come for. Three consecutive days of headlines in the "Sport" newspaper, with copious heroic images taking up several pages of the "combative, relentless" Ferdy Kübler. Hugo was practically knocked out of the paper altogether in what was a week-long Ferdy-fest. The phone rang more often, the velodromes wanted more of the man who had conquered the derby, the criterium organisers too.

Paul Egli, sat at the kitchen table in his farmhouse in Dürnten, carefully laid out his copy of the Sport newspaper and started to cut out the best photographs for his collection.

MARIANDL

Since the end of the Second World War, Austria had been under Allied occupation. A harsh winter and a poor harvest followed; people survived on a meagre diet while spending their days clearing rubble from the towns and cities that had experienced the worst of the fighting. Women were in charge, mostly. The men were still in prison camps and when they did return, they were miserable, injured and, not to put too fine a point on it, useless. It was taking the Austrians time to view themselves as a defeated nation, but they would admit to being deflated and demoralised. They would seek an escape from the hardship of those post-war years and so a new genre of film emerged known as *heimatfilm*, or 'Homeland Film'.

In these *heimatfilms*, moviegoers were transported to a world untouched by war, a world of fairy tales, love stories and rural wholesomeness. Where better to shoot the very first *heimatfilm* than the Wachau province of Austria, an idyllic region that had escaped the devastation. That film would be called *Der Hofrat Geiger* – Counsellor Geiger.

It opens with the words:

"This film is set in Austria today, which is poor and full of worry. But do not be afraid, we will show you little of that."

Der Hofrat Geiger was a roaring success, selling over 2 million tickets over the space of four years. It was also the first silver screen appearance for a young actress called Waltraut Haas. Waltraut had grown up in Linz, and performed there on stage during the war years. Her role as Mariandl in *Der Hofrat Geiger* propelled her to stardom across the German-speaking nations. She was perfect for the role – blonde, beautiful, pure as the driven snow... who better to play the role of the Counsellor Geiger's illegitimate daughter Mariandl.

Waltraut's world widened immediately. She received invites to theatres, cinemas, magazine interviews. And, bizarrely, the opportunity to present prizes to winners at bicycle races. She had no particular affection for bicycle racing, but the organisers of a criterium in Basel – Switzerland of all places – were keen to welcome Mariandl.

You would often find celebrities at the start line of bicycle races, and you would often find them at the finish line too, handing out bouquets of flowers or trophies. Josephine Baker was almost an ever-present at the start of the Tour de France before the war, and post-war you could find Orson Welles cutting the tape and discussing race tactics with riders. Sugar Ray Robinson was fighting in town one day. Where better to promote the fight than the most popular circus in town, the Tour de France. He even found time to exchange a few photographic jousts with Hugo Koblet for the gathered paparazzi. During the 1950s, it was almost impossible not to find Yvette Horner playing her accordion at a Tour stage. It was a virtuous circle – we take some of your glitz and glamour and you can access to our grit and glamour. Perhaps.

Two worlds very much keen on colliding.

The organisers of the Basel Grand Prix were looking for their own slice of celebrity for their 1951 edition. Waltraut was in town filming *Es Liegt Was In Der Luft* – There Is Something in The Air, an Austrian *heimatfilm* in which two perfume-makers produce a scent that makes a person irresistible to the opposite sex.

There is an obvious segue here.

Hugo Koblet was said to have been so seduced by Waltraut Haas as she opened affairs at the Basel Grand Prix that he told everyone on the start line that he was going to win just so that he could meet Waltraut and ask her on a date. True to his word, he won the race by a considerable distance, having the time to comb his hair, wash his face with Perrier water and dry himself down before rushing to the podium where Waltraut was waiting. Hugo didn't think this was enough of an opportunity to strike up a relationship with the actress, so thinking on his feet, he invited Waltraut to sit on the frame of his bike while he took her on a lap of honour. She sat with great discomfort on Hugo's top tube while the adoring crowds cheered the pair around the Basel velodrome.

That evening, Waltraut and Hugo went their separate ways. For many months, Hugo tried in vain to make contact with Waltraut, calling around studios and her fellow actors, trying to get her phone number. Eventually, not realising that Waltraut had a private line that was guarded with the utmost secrecy, he started looking for opportunities to race in Vienna on the off-chance that Waltraut might be in the crowd or – who knows – handing out prizes to the lucky winner. Well, who knows.

On his arrival at the hotel in Vienna, he paid a porter to find Waltraut for him. Ask around. See if she's in town. That kind of thing. Be creative. He needn't have bothered – Waltraut herself arrived at the hotel looking for Hugo. The next day, the two were a couple.

This sent the Austrian and Swiss media into a frenzy. Wherever they went, they were followed by a flickering of camera flashes, a hail of questions – Waltraut, will you be marrying Hugo at the Tour de France? Hugo, when do you plan to propose to Mariandl?

Marriage was on the cards, eventually. Hugo proposed, Waltraut accepted, and the two were engaged in 1952 with no confirmation on the actual date. Film and cycling commitments ensured that the happy couple saw less of each other than they may have wanted, Waltraut accepting no less than six roles in films that would be released in 1952 with the heavy promotion that went along with each. Hugo had returned from commitments in Mexico with an illness of some description, Waltraut could never quite identify what was wrong. She ignored the whispers about his infidelity.

As the 1953 racing season came to a premature close for Hugo, he accepted a three-month stint in Nicaragua to set up a new cycling team. He insisted Waltraut come with him, but underestimated his partner's determination to succeed in the movies, and perhaps underestimated the role of the modern Austrian woman. It had, after all, been the women of Austria who had cleared the rubble day after day while cowering in fear at night from the rapists of the Red Army. They had run households and raised children while the men were away fighting, so did they need men at all? And if given the opportunity for success, why should Waltraut take a backwards step and abandon her film commitments to follow her man for a winter in Nicaragua of all places?

Hugo tried to put his foot down. "You care for your career more than me," he moaned.

"I care for you just as much as my career," she replied. And with that, the two were no longer a couple. Hugo went to Nicaragua and returned with his tail between his legs, a failed business venture behind him. No team would be formed. Hugo was miserable, fearing for his career, and single once more.

Waltraut knew that Hugo was not ready. A child of his time, she thought. But not of mine.

Mariandl walked away.

1954

RIVALS
IN
ROMANDIE

The Tour de Romandie's reputation has grown over the past few years. The *Caravane Publicitaire* has doubled, the press is taking more of an interest and this year, there is the extra treat of the two K's. Hugo Koblet has recovered sufficiently from last year's incident at the Tour de France, and has spent the winter keeping himself fit. He returned to win Sassari-Cagliari with some style before he was expelled from Milano-Torino only for the entire peloton to go on strike in support. He was reinstated and raced to the finish.

He raced Roubaix, although you need luck to win Roubaix and he didn't have it. But then he went to the Vigorelli and he beat Fausto Coppi in the pursuit, a victory made sweeter after last year's betrayal on the Stelvio. Yes, Hugo is back, look at him fly. And fly he did, winning the Zürich Championships with such magnificence that people were comparing this vintage to that of 1951. Perhaps, some suggested, it was thanks to the love of a young lady, a model no less. Hugo could not possibly comment on tittle-tattle.

Ferdy had lined up a string of Classics for his springtime outings. Milan-San Remo didn't quite work out, but then again it never did. Gent-Wevelgem came next and Ferdy found himself marked out of the race so he told Rolf Graf to have a go, and what do you know, Rolf Graf won the race. Ferdy then raced Paris-Roubaix, a race he had always admired from afar. Hugo had come along too, but when Ferdy found himself in the front group just 18km from the velodrome, Hugo could not be found. Ferdy felt his luck was about to change.

Germain Derycke made the first move from the back of the group and Ferdy followed, but Raymond Impanis was in imperious mood that Sunday afternoon. Having already won Paris-Nice and the Tour of Flanders, he came with a fresh new reputation as a Classics man, and by the time he crossed the smooth cobblestones outside the velodrome, he was 100m ahead of Derycke who was dropping back, his legs having expired. Ferdy saw his chance for a podium place, at least, but when he banked the velodrome, two more Belgians saw their chance. Ockers, of course. Rijckaert as well. He would have to make do with fourth place but was pleased that he had at least completed the race.

The Ardennes weekend went badly, and he was beaten on the line in Paris-Bruxelles, but Ferdy was happy that he was still racing, still competing to a degree, and this augured well for the rest of the season.

The two K's left the pretty host town of Le Locle for the week-long Tour de Romandie watching each other perhaps more than they were watching the rest of the peloton. As a result of this mutual suspicion, a group escaped and was allowed to run up a 17-minute lead over the main group which included the two K's. Ferdy seemed happy that Hugo had not escaped; Hugo was visibly disappointed in how the day had panned out. Ferdy had a man in the breakaway and later informed journalists that it was his intention to neutralise the chase to the benefit of his teammate.

A developing feature of the season would be the rather vocal suggestions that Ferdy Kübler could not be trusted. Hugo's teammates called open season on Ferdy, accusing him of deliberately killing Hugo's chances on the first stage, in turn killing the whole Tour de Romandie.

This was the pattern of the week, with bitter recriminations on both sides, Hugo marking Ferdy, Ferdy marking Hugo, putting knives in each other and putting knives into Romandie. Hugo made no secret of his antipathy towards Ferdy – "he was only racing against me this week", he would complain, and was backed up by the organisers for whom the Tour was a huge disappointment. They had been banking on a battle of the two K's, and instead had to make do with Jean Forestier and Pasquale Fornara battling it out for the lead, to the disinterest of many.

It was perhaps wise of Ferdy to withdraw himself from consideration for the Giro d'Italia, then. Much was against him. Age, for one. He was now 34, going on 35. Rösli was expecting him to be home more often, to focus on shorter races and, who knows, a post-racing career. Fatherhood, in particular. Ferdy had chosen a specific end-of-career pathway – not that of the wise head of the peloton, not that of a future team director like Hans Martin – no, Ferdy was going to focus on 'brand Ferdy'. Get that massive nose out there more often. Make people remember your name, because when it's on billboards, it has to mean something.

His isolation meant that riders lined up against him. Even Emilio Croci-Torti had switched allegiances, and he had been Ferdy's most loyal lieutenant of all.

So the Giro was not on Ferdy's calendar, and besides, the organisers had made it quite clear that after his antics of 1953, Ferdy wouldn't be welcome anyway. Nobody wants a quitter and nobody abandons the Italians' adopted Christ-on-a-bike, the so-called "Super Koblet", at least according to the Gazzeta dello Sport who railed against "that other K", the K they didn't like quite as much.

This Giro was, like most Giros, all about Fausto Coppi. And not just in bicycling terms. The winner of last year's Giro was now an adulterer. Even the Pope had an opinion on Fausto Coppi's extra-marital affair with *la dama bianca*, although the minute Fausto sat on a bike, all was forgiven. By some. Temporarily.

For those more interested in racing than tittle-tattle, this year's Giro had an extra flavour that would transform some of the action. For the first time, intermediate sprint points would be awarded throughout stages, which meant that the likes of Rik van Steenbergen could participate in the first 200km of a stage rather than just the final 2km. This is indeed what took place on the 5th stage between Bari and Naples – van Steenbergen and the Dutchman Gerrit Voorting took it upon themselves to liven affairs and take as many points as they could throughout the day, even up to the finish line where Voorting took the pink jersey. It was exciting, but nobody cared too much as the race would only come to life in the latter stages, surely.

If anything, this stage ought to have been a warning for the GC favourites Coppi, Magni and Koblet, who had spent the day languishing in the peloton allowing the sprinters to play for a different colour of jersey. The introduction of sprint points had transformed stages, and if the wrong men were ever to escape one day, they might never be caught.

The next morning, the Giro departed from Naples in the direction of l'Aquila in intense heat. Riders like Voorting and van Steenbergen had given their all the previous day and spent the day recovering with their teammates while a breakaway of seeming non-entities escaped after 32km. They included two Swiss riders, Martin Metzger and Carlo Clerici, as well as a Belgian – Petters, a Dutchman – Roks, and an Italian – Assirelli. Better to let them have their day in the sunshine – none of them are a threat to the pink jersey, and none would figure in the points competition.

However, as the day grew longer, the gap grew wider. Once the breakaway tasted fresher temperatures in the Liri valley, the riders had racked up an astonishing 21-minute lead over the main group. Coppi, who had lost over 11 minutes to Clerici on the second stage, appeared not to have the legs to challenge. Hugo found himself in the unusual position of controlling the peloton with a teammate so far ahead. The gap grew to 39 minutes and when Carlo Clerici won the sprint in the velodrome, they had to convince him they weren't joking when they gave him the *maglia rosa*.

The conclusion was that this stage was a grave error. A stupid mistake. The Giro was over already due to tactical stupor. A half-witted peloton baked in the early morning sunshine while an astute breakaway built up an unassailable lead. Not one of the riders up ahead believed that they would achieve such a margin, and not one of the riders behind believed the numbers they were shown.

The result of this apathy? A nobody would win the Giro. A man nobody had ever heard of.

And so Hugo devoted himself to Carlo's Giro, forming the 'red legion' and riding hard day-in, day-out to protect their *maglia rosa*. The Italians would blame Coppi for lacking the attention required to defend a Giro, they would blame the white lady for distracting him from his family and his sport, and belatedly they would accept that Fausto Coppi's time had probably been and gone, and a new generation would need time to develop, time to learn their trade.

There was still time for Fausto to win in Bolzano, as per the tradition, and there was still time for Hugo to win the time trial, also as per tradition. There was even time for the riders to stage a go-slow strike on the stage out of Bolzano into Saint-Moritz. The remaining 67 riders went over the Bernina as if it were a Sunday club ride. Why today, of all days, had they chosen to do this? Perhaps in protest at the overly lengthy Giro, its punishing schedule which was out of line with modern races and their shorter stages. Perhaps they were bored.

The Italians – who had organised the strike – would pay for it later on with exclusion from the Tour de France, but the red legion returned to Switzerland triumphant. Hugo had put aside all notions of winning a second Giro after that 6th stage and instead worked relentlessly alongside his team members to ensure that the *maglia rosa* would be worn by a Swiss rider for the second time at the end of a Giro. Rapturous write-ups would focus not necessarily on Clerici but the selfless, magnificent Hugo. How wonderful he is, they noted, sacrificing his own chances for a teammate. In parentheses, a lesser rider.

It is often at moments like these that Ferdy Kübler is at his most irritable. 8,000 spectators flocked to the Oerlikon velodrome to welcome home the magnificent seven and watch their heroes perform in an Omnium. Ferdy made it eight, but he struggled to maintain even the most basic level of sincerity in his congratulations to Carlo and Hugo. He tightened his laces, mounted his bike and won the Omnium in brutal style, crushing the tired heroes of the Giro in a manner that said "don't you dare forget about Ferdy."

Hugo made it very clear to Alex Burtin that afternoon that under no circumstances would he allow Ferdy Kübler to join his team at the Tour de France. After all, Ferdy had been told to stay away by the organisers of the Giro. He had humiliated his fellow riders at the Oerlikon and earlier in the season he had neutralised Romandie to prevent a Koblet victory. Better then to select the Magnificent Seven and use the extra three slots the Swiss team were afforded at the Tour for some younger blood – perhaps Hans Hollenstein? Selecting Ferdy Kübler would only sow division and cause trouble within a team that had developed a bond without him.

Alex Burtin was easily persuaded. He thought back to 1950, his first Tour, and the effort required to build a team around Ferdy, the coaxing and the cajoling. And then he thought of 1951, and how easy it seemed in comparison. Hugo was right, Ferdy was getting on in age, and getting cranky with it.

Ferdy sunk into a depression. The team didn't want him, and yet there were plenty of fans who wanted to see Ferdy try to win the Tour one last time. The Café Rio in Lausanne would overspill with loyal Kübleristes exchanging conspiracy theories.

Rumours flew around Hans Martin's nearby pro-Koblet Schutzen restaurant that the Kübleristes were planning to sabotage the Swiss National Championships, and naturally Ferdy won that title in a sprint against Schär, Clerici and Koblet. There would be no sabotage, but the pro-Koblet "Sport" newspaper found its car pelted with stones as it followed the race. Kübleristes wrote to local and national newspapers and sang pro-Kübler songs all night at the Café Rio as if this were a political rally, as if this were more than just cycling.

Positions had hardened over the years. There were many in Switzerland who disapproved of Hugo's playboy lifestyle, and who in contrast approved wholeheartedly of Ferdy's wholesome Swiss values. It was of little importance to them that Ferdy had isolated himself from his fellow riders, they were all wrong and Ferdy was right.

Across the road at the Schutzen, the Kobletistes played jazz and partied long into the night. There would be no chanting, no writing to newspapers and no pelting of stones. The world is moving on, and if these people can't understand, well it's their loss.

On a practical level, however, this couldn't continue. Hugo agreed to a summit, held by Carl Senn who was still the President of the Swiss Cycling Federation. Ferdy would agree, in writing, to support Hugo's attempt to win his second Tour de France. Ferdy argued for the insertion of a specific clauses – that he would agree to ride as *domestique* for Hugo

"... if Hugo were to display the form and capability to fulfil his ambitions."

Clause or no clause, it was further humiliation for Ferdy. He had to swallow his pride to race with a team that no longer trusted him and no longer wanted him.

But he would be able to ride the Tour after all.

THE TOUR
OF THE
TWO K'S

Ahhh, *le Bel Hugo,* enthused André Leducq in his Miroir des Sports column. He is *le Bel Hugo* from 1951 once more. If Louison were able to beat *le Bel Hugo*, he'd have plenty of tales to tell his grandchildren.

André hasn't really followed the Classics season this year. He admits that he rarely does, but he's a man of the world, and a man who understands cycling. He has no need to watch these races; he reads the report and understands better than anyone – so he says – who is in form and who is not. And *le Bel Hugo* is indeed in form, whether he has been getting the results he wanted or not.

André reflects that 1953 had been a year of tactical errors for *le Bel Hugo.* Firstly, allowing Fausto Coppi to dominate him in the Dolomites, both physically and psychologically, and secondly by attacking on the Aubisque when he was already on his limit. But *le Bel Hugo* is an intelligent man, and he will have learned from his mistakes in 1953. We can only hope that bad luck does not come in threes and that Hugo is a more astute rider this year.

And just imagine what a wiser, more tactically competent Hugo could achieve! A Koblet who is satisfied with consistency, a regular presence on the front of the pack, controlling breakaways and managing his effort throughout! How dangerous could he be were he to manage a race and win time trials, take time bonuses wherever possible. If he could add this layer to the natural gifts that God has given him, ahhhh, *le Bel Hugo*, he could win this Tour with his eyes closed.

Hugo may not have read Miroir des Sports, given his attack just 74km into the first stage out of Amsterdam. Schär and Ferdy himself joined Hugo on a breakaway, soon discovering they were nine minutes ahead of a peloton that had barely realised the Tour de France was underway.

Ferdy may have dreamed of competing for the overall victory himself but a puncture put paid to those hopes and he dropped back into the peloton and committed himself to controlling the pace, not that it needed controlling.

In stage two, Hugo and Ferdy both escaped alongside Louison Bobet. Ferdy was leading out Hugo for a sprint, but his foot appeared to slip from his toe-clips, and he dropped back suddenly. Louison saw the opportunity to attack and put a gap between himself and Hugo. For Hugo the opportunity had gone, but for Ferdy, foot back in toe-clip, there was still a chance for second. Instinctively, he took it, nearly beating Louison on the line, but in the process denying Hugo the bonus seconds. As a consequence, Hugo would be a full minute behind Louison in the general classification.

Ferdy returned to furious accusations and finger pointing from the Kobletistes in the Swiss team, which was almost all of them. Alex Burtin intervened to remind all that Ferdy was here to work for Hugo and had Ferdy not worked so hard throughout the day, Hugo may not even have come third. Therefore, we are one team, we work for one man. There is no more to say.

More would be said once Alex Burtin had left the room. Ferdy could not be trusted.

Hugo attacked again on stage three between Lille and Rouen. Taking the Cote de Doullens at a speed of 40km per hour, he left the peloton struggling to recover the gap. Could it be another Brive-Agens, wondered André Leducq, pen poised at the ready for another lengthy homage to *le Bel Hugo*. Write my words for me, Hugo. Alas, not today. He was caught and finished with the group in 10th place.

There was a team time trial on the Essarts motor racing circuit, and that went entirely to plan with Hugo and Fritz Schär finishing together for the stage win, pushing Hugo up the general classification into third place.

As the Tour wound its way anti-clockwise around France, the Swiss tactics were leaving a mark on their rivals. Raphaël Géminiani complained: "if we're forced to chase these white crosses every day, I'm going to need the Red Cross."

Louison Bobet, wearing yellow in his native Brittany, found himself at the back of the peloton while news went round that the two K's had gone off the front again alongside Croci-Torti. The three white crosses relayed furiously over the hills and through the dips of the Breton countryside while Bobet burned matchsticks and teammates, eventually pulling off a sensational pursuit thanks to help from his tiny colleague Bergaud.

Hugo looked over his shoulder and puffed out his cheeks in admiration.

"Louison, you made it here with just this little fella?"

Bobet nodded.

"That's impressive. Seriously impressive."

After a further stage chasing white crosses across the French countryside, the French team held an emergency summit where it was decided that they would abandon the yellow jersey. Raphaël Géminiani in particular was in favour of taking the target off Louison's back. If the two K's are going to run us into the ground every day, we won't even make it to the Pyrenees. Maybe we should let a Belgian or a Dutchman take up the slack? Wout Wagtmans duly took up the aforementioned slack on the stage between Vannes and Angers. Hugo knew the game, however, and as Bobet and team allowed Wagtmans to slip away and build up an advantage, he encouraged Louison to keep the gap down to something that he could retrieve sooner rather than later.

Louison showed his gratitude, but Koblet attacked him the very next day, forcing him into another energy-sapping pursuit ahead of the Pyrenees. It didn't matter who was wearing yellow, the Swiss strategy was to wear out Bobet at all costs.

Stage 10 from Bordeaux to Bayonne was a flat stage, a chance for the sprinters to have their day and shouldn't have posed problems to the Swiss team or indeed to any team. After just 47km though, two Dutchmen collided. Ferdy, switching to avoid them, makes contact with Hugo's wheel, bringing Hugo down along with several other riders. At first, it just felt like any other crash. A few men got up, dusted themselves down and thought about getting back into the race. Hugo's shorts were ripped, however, his leg bloodied. Every Swiss rider – including Ferdy – stopped to haul Hugo back on his bike.

André Darrigade later recounted:

"Hugo then rode at an insane pace. The speed he was riding at, hardly any of his team could keep up with him. Maybe Ferdy, from time to time. This was 40km per hour all the way, barely taking his hands off the drops. But he was suffering. Really suffering. This was an achievement the like of which I've never seen before."

L'Equipe had sent a new journalist down to Bayonne that day, a certain Antoine Blondin. Covering the first day of his very first Tour, Blondin marvelled at the rituals of the Tour, its *caravane* of hangers-on and *gendarmes*, the cast of superstars accompanying a cast of journalists and writers, sports halls transformed into *salles de rédaction* where reporters filed their pieces to the smell of Nescafé.

He wrote:

"The news came late morning – Madam is dead! Madam is dead! And for an instant, we were left suspended in momentary horror, like an upper-class lady who realises she has left her diamond necklace in the toilet. But history will tell you of how Hugo Koblet fought back with the help of Ferdy Kübler – both demon and angel – battling as never before."

Hugo crossed the finish line and continued past Blondin, past Leducq and past the other journalists, straight to the hotel where his soigneur awaited him, bandages and all. His injuries were more than superficial, and his team made sure to stress that his muscles were working perfectly fine, even if Hugo looked like an Egyptian mummy.

Hugo spent the night in agony, Ferdy at his side.

There is a photograph of Ferdy, himself with plasters on his elbow, attending to the bed-ridden Hugo Koblet. It is a picture in perfect contrast with the atmosphere surrounding the Swiss team ahead of this race. Had Ferdy found peace as a *domestique*? Had the two K's actually found friendship? They were smiling in the photograph, not for the camera but for each other. Had we all been played for fools?

The next morning, Hugo approached the journalists with a smile on his face, chattier than usual as if believing an excess of words could patch over the nightmare of the last 24 hours.

"I fell like an amateur, despite being at the front of the peloton where really I should have been safe. From what I remember, I was thrown towards Ferdy who is a far better acrobat than I. He managed to stay upright and then came straight back to help me out. I would have been fine were it not for a number of riders who fell on top of me. I received a knee to my head which nearly knocked me out. When I came round, the peloton had long gone – I assume, seeking an advantage over me."

Pain is inescapable. You can try to smile it away. Often, you can ride it away, using the repetition to lull your body into a false sense of security. Mostly though, pain seeps from the cuts and the grazes into the marrow of your bones. It is your constant companion, parroting away on your shoulder. You can try to transfer the pain into the bicycle, you look for tiny increments of comfort that can chip away at it. And then you give in to it.

Hugo couldn't smile away the pain. His arrival into Pau was nearly two full minutes behind the leading group, and the next day he fought against the gradients, zig-zagging to reduce a 10% gradient down to 7%, fighting to keep his bike upright as gravity fought to pull him backwards. He finished 27 minutes behind the leading group and was now 31 minutes behind the new yellow jersey, Gilbert Bauvin. Of all people, Gilbert Bauvin.

The end of the road was coming for Hugo.

Jacques Goddet, writing in l'Equipe, wrote:

"The drama began at the foot of the Tourmalet.

In that moment, at the start of what would be 18km of climbing, a group of red jerseys slipped out of the peloton, losing contact and advancing at a ridiculously slow speed, akin to that of the cyclo-tourist. The robust torsos of the loyal Croci-Torti, his lookalike Huber, Pianezzi too, could not hide the sudden distress of the comrade they were surrounding, the Apollo-on-a-bike that is Hugo Koblet. The *Pedaleur de Charme*, this poor man, pedalling squares, his eyes vacant, brutally cut from the race. You could hear him murmuring to himself – I don't have the legs, I don't have the legs. In just four kilometres, he had lost six minutes. It was at the same time tragic and pathetic. And yet Hugo rode on, as if he had lost all sensation, through this calvary. What dignity he showed, a man bandaged across his legs, his elbows, his face daubed in antiseptic."

The gap continued to grow. The following cars appeared embarrassed to leave Hugo and his friends to their sad fate, apologising as they accelerated away. We have a race to get to.

Hugo fought on up the Tourmalet at a pace no faster than that of a village postman, his pale face dripping with sweat, his eyes boring into the distance.

And yet, freed from the prying eyes of photographers, freed from the humiliation of the watching drivers unable to maintain his ponderous pace without stopping and starting again, Hugo slowly regained a cadence that would help him crest the Tourmalet. Little by little, with the help of his team, Hugo fought against himself. Right leg, left leg, right leg, left leg, thinking in small numbers, count to four and count again, don't look up at the mountain, take it in small chunks. There was no encouragement from the men around him, no words would help now, this was about silently chewing up small parts of road and getting Hugo home, getting him into Luchon within the time limit. Some were reminded of Fausto's spectacular defaillance in 1951 on the road to Montpellier, and yet Fausto got home that day. Hugo would do the same.

Hugo had agreed to be ordinary that day. To appear less majestic. He found within himself a victory that may ultimately matter more than any Grand Tour, Classic or week-long stage race that he may have dominated in previous years – a victory over himself. He had lost his lustre, he had seen lesser men ride away from him without so much as turning their heads, and he had accepted it with meek humiliation. Ockers, Bobet, Wagtmans, eventually Schär and Kübler – each with their own battle plan, each sent ahead with a sigh and an acknowledgement that the Koblet of old, the *pedaleur de charme* is without charme, and can barely *pedaler*.

That he made it to the finish line that afternoon was an accomplishment, but not one that he would be able to repeat the next day. The peloton almost willed Hugo to remain within, slowing as one to suck him back into their fold, but try as they might, *le Bel Hugo* could not be retained.

It was in Masseube, a small village in Armagnac-Bigorre, just 100m from the Claverie family farm, that Hugo slowed down to a crawl, then to a stop, and climbed from his bike. He propped himself up against the bike, a beaten man. Tears fell from his eyes, his face ravaged with pain and relief at no longer having to propel himself forward. Bandages fell from his arms. Team cars insensitively dawdled past at walking pace to catch a glimpse of the great Hugo Koblet. Photographers circled like vultures, they just couldn't resist, looking for angles at which to capture their prey. And yet there Hugo remained for many minutes, immobile, the only movement the up and down sway of his chest. Teammate Marcel Huber remained alongside. He was soon sent away only to ride two more kilometres himself before quitting the race entirely. Martin Metzger did likewise.

Hugo pulled himself up straight and acknowledged his audience, before climbing into the ambulance which had been waiting for him, as if it had known from the first kilometre that it would be welcoming *le Bel Hugo*. A young reporter climbed in alongside him, handed him a bidon filled with lemonade. Hugo drank a short mouthful and handed it back. He looked the reporter up and down and sighed.

"You need some words. OK. I feel fine. And yet I've lost all strength. From the moment I fell on the Bayonne-Pau stage, I could barely move my legs. I had a terrible time in the mountains between Pau and Luchon, but I wanted to hold on because I thought I would come back. I had to accept the terrible truth today that it wasn't going to happen.

My muscles were no longer listening to me."

The girls of Toulouse could close their shutters and return inside from the heat of their balconies. *Le Bel Hugo* would not pass by as promised. His Tour was over.

It was on the climb of the Tourmalet that Ferdy had offered his support to Hugo, dropping in to provide a wheel. But Hugo insisted that Ferdy go on ahead. And Ferdy, while not the Ferdy of 1950, had found some climbing legs. By this point, Ferdy had earned the green jersey, a recent introduction for the leader in the points competition. After Hugo's abandonment, the Swiss team were down to just six men and the atmosphere at the evening table was – to put it mildly – morose.

Ferdy didn't have much support. As he settled down for the evening in his hotel room in Millau, he received a knock at the door. Three men stood at that door – Clerici, Pianezzi and Croci-Torti. They rejected the offer to come inside, and instead sheepishly held out a piece of paper on which they had scribbled the word 'contract', and the following stipulations – that the riders would only support Ferdy as team leader if he were to surrender all bonuses to them – in other words, all individual, team and points bonuses. Furthermore, they accused Ferdy of trying to sell the 'Challenge Martini' – the team competition – to the French, in exchange for the green jersey. The only way to prevent Ferdy from arranging his own deals, they claimed, was to fix Ferdy himself.

This hurt Ferdy immensely. Clerici and Pianezzi he could understand – they were hardcore Kobletistes. But Emilio had been by his side for many years, shielding him from the wind, giving him a slipstream, even cooking him breakfast. The fact that his best friend no longer trusted him was a stab in the back, and perhaps one that Ferdy never truly recovered from. Nevertheless, Ferdy signed the contract and the next day, attacked Louison from the off with a sparkling attack and a devilish descent, growing the Red Legion's gap over the French team to 20 points.

As a competition, the Tour was more or less decided even before Louison Bobet added to his growing legend over Izoard. Ferdy fell behind in the *casse déserte*, just ahead of the summit, finishing 2nd on the stage to Louison and ensuring that he would keep his green points jersey.

There were still suspicions within the team that Ferdy had made deals with the French team. Remo Pianezzi was convinced Ferdy had sold the team competition to the French. On the penultimate stage, with Louison Bobet struggling to maintain the pace, Pianezzi was calling for his team leader to attack. Instead, Ferdy sat up and started to complain about the cold weather and the rain. Why not attack? What the hell are you doing, Ferdy? If not now, when?

Of course, Ferdy had made an agreement. It was a 'pact of non-aggression' struck with Louison, to simply help him get to the finish without any mishap. Well, Ferdy thought, if you want me to sign your stupid contract, I'll find something to my advantage somewhere else. Pact or no pact, Louison kept the pace in the end, won the time trial and therefore the whole Tour by a distance. Ferdy came second overall and kept the green jersey while the remaining Swiss riders celebrated the Challenge Martini, and for the third time, Ferdy Kübler won the Desgrange-Colombo challenge for the best rider of the year.

A good vintage, he thought. But one that left a bad taste.

HUGO: *I don't remember if you ever abandoned a race, Ferdy. Did you? If not, I can tell you, it's far easier to give up on a flat road than on a mountain. I am here now, in Armagnac country, on roads that practically pull you along they're so flat and smooth, and the time has come. I could have abandoned the race yesterday on the mountain, but what man quits on a climb? A climb can bruise you and break you until you are half the man you ever were, but it's there to be overcome. A flat road leaves you exposed.*

I'm hanging by a thread, Ferdy. I have nothing to overcome other than my own weakness. Bandages will come off eventually. Cuts and grazes will heal. Headaches will dissipate. But this race has left me behind, waved goodbye long ago, wished me luck and hoped I'll recover. I still have my boys with me – Marcel to one side, Martin the other. They haven't spoken for over an hour.

The question isn't whether to quit, it's when. It's a process. You have to reach the point of no return, you have to commit to quitting. I've been thinking about it for too long, dismissing it as an option reserved for weak men. But there comes a point where you tip from hope to no-hope, where it becomes clear you don't have the strength of other men, the strength you used to have, and all the other possibilities are closed to you.

This moment doesn't appear like God descending from the clouds in a burst of light. It's an internal tussle, a debate raging inside your mind with a devil on one shoulder, an angel on the other. Ride on, boy – no, you have to quit – oh you can do it – but they're all laughing at you... this battle rages until either angel or demon is vanquished. Committing to quitting is work.

And then you must carry out the act. You look for the right reason to quit. Who can forgive you for quitting when you're injured, you can exaggerate this or that injury to your teammates and the journalists. You can justify quitting when you're on your last legs. You can justify quitting if you're dragging down your teammates. I sent you ahead, didn't I. I should never have made you sign that piece of paper – it should have been the other way round.

Quitting mid-stage is a perverse act of vanity. I could have gone in the quiet of the night, stealing away with my suitcases in the car. I could have been home by now, but instead, here I am having started the stage this morning with a modicum of hope, and all I'm looking for is the right place to bring the bicycle to a stop and to climb off and I swear, Ferdy, it's the bravest thing a rider can do.

We are brought up on the idea that our bodies are our lives, that we depend on having the fittest, strongest bodies and that we are infallible, always improving, always getting better. The sport demands that we grit our teeth and persevere. But when you visibly accept that you have nothing more to give when the world is accustomed to taking from you, this takes more courage than I had ever believed.

And still, you go through the motions of withdrawing from the race, you remove your shoes from your toe-clips and you slide from your machine, and you're still thinking – if I catch my breath perhaps I can ride on. Get to the finish. Sleep it off. But no, not this time.

The pain is echoing through every wound, my head is spiralling and my breath short and hard. I'm bent over my bicycle with the birdsong and the breeze, the click-whirr-click of photographers, the pat-pat of assorted well-wishers who have nothing left to say. There's the ominous slowing down of a vehicle, the clack-clack of a car door and the Tour's grim reaper has come for me. The broom wagon is waiting for my bicycle, the ambulance for my body. My decision has been made and the final act is the ultimate humiliation and the ultimate relief. Everyone waits. The birds sing.

Bike racing is easy, Ferdy. It's the giving up that's hard.

THE END
OF THE
ROAD

A CASE
OF MISTAKEN
IDENTITY

Sonja Buhl had been invited to the Oerlikon velodrome for a photo shoot with a cyclist, she couldn't remember which one but was pretty sure his name began with K. It must be Ferdy Kübler because, after all, who doesn't know Ferdy Kübler. Her parents talked about nothing else at the breakfast table, it was Ferdy this, Ferdy that. Ferdy Nationale, oh... her father would say, he is the greatest. A good, wholesome man. A family man. A Swiss man. Married a good girl your age, Sonja, and he looks after her and his family. Ahh, Ferdy Kübler.

Ferdy seemed a little more handsome than they had described him. That famous nose was perhaps smaller than she had at first imagined it would be. Indeed, she was a little surprised after all the descriptions she had heard of Ferdy that he had been invited to model alongside her at the Oerlikon in the first place.

And the Oerlikon of all places, what a peculiar concrete bowl, what a strange place to hold a fashion shoot. Still, they say that cyclists are all the rage. What would Sonja know, she doesn't read the sports pages of the newspapers, why should she. So she had no idea what Ferdy Kübler looked like. Just a little 'unkempt', her father would say. Big nose. Unkempt. Not a model.

He was quite professional, too. Handsome, as well. The photos that were taken that morning were going to turn out just fine. Look over there and point, said the photographer, and Ferdy pointed, and Sonja laughed, and the photo was taken and they both held their smiles.

She thought of returning to her father and telling him that Ferdy was quite charming.

He was a little persistent though. Not only did he devour her with his eyes throughout the shoot, he offered her coffee. In a café. Together, alone. Well, Ferdy Kübler, she thought – I have one thing to say to you – I never date married men!

And with that, Sonja Buhl showed her back to the cyclist called Ferdy Kübler and stormed off down the tunnel because that's what models do, and she knew that Ferdy would be devouring her back with his eyes, working his way up from her ankles, because that's what men do. Married men. Disgusting.

This cyclist, of course, was not Ferdy. This was Hugo Koblet, winner of the Giro d'Italia, winner of the Tour de France, Swiss National Pursuit Champion more times than you could mention.

Sonja Buhl didn't read the sports pages.

Hugo devoured her from the ankles upwards until she disappeared down the steps and thought to himself – married man? What? But Waltraut and I were barely even engaged. Only later did it strike him that Sonja was thinking of the other K and Hugo laughed, because what else can you do when someone mistakes you for Ferdy Kübler.

Hugo persisted. Wherever Miss Buhl went, flowers would follow. A telegram too. Dear Miss Buhl STOP – I am not married – STOP – I am not Ferdy Kübler – STOP – yours, Hugo Koblet. STOP.

Hugo did not stop, and Sonja Buhl became first Hugo's girlfriend, then Hugo's fiancée and in no short time, she became Hugo's wife. Put the happy couple on the cover of a magazine and it would sell out in a matter of hours. Hugo and Sonja were the talk of the town – wherever they went, photographers went too. When they married, the whole of Zürich would cascade from apartments into the roads, slowing the progress of the wedding car, slapping the back window as is tradition, with cries of *Sonja und Hugie* ringing out through the city. They walked between the raised wheels of cyclists from the RVZ, they took the acclamation of friends, of colleagues, even of Ferdy Kübler who had worn his best suit for the day.

They bought a villa in Forch overlooking Lake Zürich and Hugo threw money into its renovation. He was now 30 years old and perhaps the final piece of the jigsaw of his own life had been put into place. He was happy, deeply in love with his wife, and extremely rich. Perhaps, journalists mused in puff pieces, this is just what Hugo needs in order to find his form once more – the form that brought him so many victories as a young man – he just needed a wife.

And a little luck, too. Roger Bastide wrote:

"The Koblet of 1951 struck everyone by his insolent grace. He gave the impression of having been carved from a different mould than the rest of us, he was born to ride a bike and he was unbeatable. His new face bears the wounds of ill fortune, it makes him more accessible to the rest of us, brings him closer to the many admirers who continue to believe blindly in him. All Hugo needs is for the Witch With Green Teeth to give him a break."

Perhaps marriage had changed Hugo. As he climbed back on his bike for the start of the 1955 season, he took the unusual decision to race the spring Classics in northern Europe. In Flanders, he finished 2nd behind Louison Bobet, but all anyone in Geraardsbergen could talk about was how Hugo Koblet broke away on the Muur, of how good he looked and how they all wished him well.

A week later he got into an early breakaway in Paris-Roubaix, and when that dissolved, he stayed at the front of affairs where things were safer. As the rain fell and the mud splattered into the faces of Hugo and the other riders, smaller groups formed just handfuls of seconds apart. And yet he rode alongside Fausto Coppi, staying upright at 50km per hour, forcing the pace until only Jean Forestier could break his spirit. He finished 7th, just 42 seconds behind the winner, but once more all anyone could talk about was how the *Pedaleur de Charme*, *le Bel Hugo* had returned.

Hugo returned to Switzerland for Romandie, only to find the first climb too hard, losing ground on the very first morning at the very first sign of a gradient. He dominated the time trial as expected but the next day could barely haul his body over the col de Pillon, meekly submitting to gravity.

He secretly harboured hopes of a revival in the Giro d'Italia, but this was far-fetched and over-ambitious. Once more, a gradient was his undoing in the second stage, and he crossed the finish line eight minutes down on the leader. Not to worry, he thought, I could win it on time trials alone, but even then he finished fifth on the first time trial and spent the rest of the Giro with the pack, looking for support on the climbs and hoping for something better than anonymity.

Form was slipping through Hugo's fingers. It would come, occasionally. He won the Tour de Suisse although would hear nothing of those who criticised him for being unable to follow young Hans Hollenstein's wheel on the Klausen. Ferdy's bloody Klausen, why is it always the Klausen.

"I didn't judge it necessary," he told reporters afterwards. It wasn't necessary, no, not in the context of the race, but in the context of being Hugo, of being more Hugo, it was necessary to follow Hollenstein. Winning the Tour de Suisse, perversely, exposed Hugo's loss of form and hinted at a more permanent loss of ability.

What he did still have was his name. He had a wife, he had money, he had velodrome contacts coming through the letterbox almost daily. But little by little, Hugo was withdrawing into the peloton, pulled along by his colleagues in the hope that time trialling might save him.

Even victory in the Tour of Ticino could not prevent the feeling that Hugo had prematurely become yesterday's man at the tender age of 30, an age at which other riders had come into their prime. Riders like Ferdy Kübler, if anyone dare mention his name in Hugo's presence.

Hugo was now inspired to race harder at the very thought of Ferdy. He rode away from him in the Swiss Road Championships, taking the title ahead of Metzger, Clerici and that pesky Hollenstein. Some said that Hugo's win here was merely representative of a downturn in Swiss cycling fortunes, as opposed to an upturn in Hugo's.

Hugo withdrew from consideration for the Tour de France, citing injuries from previous years that prevented him from competing at the highest level. He spent much of his summer either at home or competing in criteriums. After all, those renovations won't pay for themselves and criteriums pay well. There was never a shortage in takers for the name that is Hugo Koblet.

They'd just have to make do with the Hugo Koblet of today, not the one from 5 years ago.

VENTOUX

Mont Ventoux is not a new mountain. It has always been there, even before the Tour de France discovered it in 1951, like Columbus discovering America. Look, people, look what we have found! If you venture a little towards the centre of France, there is a new mountain, one we have never seen before.

No, Mont Ventoux stands there as if it pre-dates time itself. Wind-blown and bald like Fiorenzo Magni made of rock, it stands wrapped in a shawl of trees within the Massif Central, ready to lure cyclists into its trap before they realise it's too late and they're at the mercy of nature and there is quite literally no way out.

You approach from Bedoin, a small, ageless village surrounded by trees and fields of ochre. You feel the burning in your legs and your lungs as you rise through forests, capturing glimpses of sun through the trees. Before long, those trees brutally take their leave and you are alone with nature. She could be windy, she could be burning hot, she could be both. It depends on her mood that day. Mont Ventoux, she is capricious.

Riders had of course been taking on the mountain for many years. There were competitions dating back as far as 1905 in which riders would take over two hours to cover the 19km to the summit. They called it the Mont Ventoux Marathon, which was technically a misnomer, but it played to the spirit of the competition.

In '51 and '52, they brought the Tour de France inland to Ventoux, a temporary incursion away from the coast as they discovered la France profonde, that mysterious void between east and west, between north and south, and in doing so they discovered that people would still line the streets for the Tour, that there was something new to revive and refresh the race. Now they had ventured this far inland, even though it really wasn't that far inland, the Tour would change forever.

The '55 Tour returns to Ventoux with further change in the air. The glory days of Swiss cycling are behind us. Last year's Giro seems an aberration given the state of Hugo Koblet these days, and he has given way to youth, or at least so he says. His doctor says that he's suffering from lesions to his vertebrae, caused by several falls last year, so whether he cedes to youth or a bad back, it doesn't really matter. Hugo will not race.

Ferdy Kübler is there, for what it's worth. He turns

36 in a matter of weeks and has none of the spark that would both frighten and amuse a peloton in his heyday. Once upon a time, he would turn around and yell "Ferdy is lighting the fire today boys, just watch Ferdy ride!" and off he would ride, soaking up the laughter which died the minute they realised he was serious.

This is not to say that Ferdy doesn't come with ambition of some description. Last year's green points jersey showed that he can still play a role, and he wanted to demonstrate this on the early stage between Colmar and Zürich. He attacked in Basel with only Pasquale Fornara able to follow him, but a group including André Darrigade was soon to make contact. Once they did, Darrigade refused to take any turns on the front, causing Ferdy to turn round and spit – "What the hell are you doing? Do some work on the front boy!" but Darrigade pretended not to hear Ferdy. Tsk, kids these days.

For over 50km, Darrigade sat behind Ferdy's wheel while Ferdy launched attack after explosive attack, his back arched, his nose almost touching his front wheel. Darrigade remained impassive, seeking the most aerodynamic position he could find, flattening himself out as the wind blew, as Ferdy tried to put the knife into him. Each time, the sun-tanned young Frenchman would bridge the gap.

They entered the Oerlikon velodrome, the velodrome in which 16 years previously, Ferdy had become the next big thing and had acted as a catalyst for that Golden Era of Swiss road cycling. André Darrigade overtook him and won the stage with absolutely no grace, absolutely no respect, absolutely no thought of what it might have meant for Ferdy Kübler to have won this stage in his home velodrome. He took a victory lap to the boos of the locals while Ferdy, red-faced and distraught, sat in tears as the crowd yelled 'Hop Ferdy's to raise his spirits.

A young rider called Charly Gaul showed him equally little respect on the Galibier, beating Ferdy into second place, when really he should have allowed Ferdy one final victory in the mountains, because surely Charly Gaul would have many victories in the future anyway. Tsk, kids these days.

On the 18th July, the Tour would dip inland and visit the now famous, newly rediscovered Mont Ventoux. It would be the third time that Ventoux had featured in the race, but the first time that Ferdy would climb it. In total there would be 1,600m of climbing, going east to west over the mountain and back down into Avignon. The temperature had been climbing too. A heatwave is customary on the Tour, but a heatwave on Ventoux...

Ferdy escaped early, rolling back the years in his quest for a second green jersey and as many points as he could take. Together with Raphaël Géminiani, he passed through Bedoin at high speed. Legend has it the two riders exchanged words, with Géminiani telling Ferdy:

"Be careful, Ventoux is a mountain not like any other."

In response, according to legend, Ferdy would

reply, "Yes, and Ferdy is a Champion not like any other."

If this were true – and both riders would later deny it – it did not stop Géminiani from responding to Ferdy Kübler's attacks up the forested slopes of Ventoux. At least here, there is shade, some relief from the beating sun. Their advantage grew to 1'15" over a peloton that included Louison Bobet, and had grown a further 15 seconds once they reached Chalet Reynard.

It is after Chalet Reynard that Ventoux removes its coat of cedar, beech and juniper and reveals its naked fury. Riders are exposed to the elements, whatever they might be that day. Wind, usually, but today a 38-degree furnace on a climb that averages out at 7.5%. And that includes the easy bit at the bottom.

Ferdy could see Géminiani getting away, not because the Frenchman had gone on the attack, but because his body was starting to shut down. In response, he asked for more from his legs, hammering away at the pedals, but no response came from the machine below him. He lurched from left to right in vain, a rider in slow motion.

There are times during which a rider battles his uncertainty, searches for what's coming next. They can be momentary blips, little understood but fleeting. Or they can be transformational, turning a whole race upside down. During the time it took Ferdy to realise that it was the latter, his body was revolting against him for the final time. Raphaël

Géminiani had turned into miniature in the distance like one of those metal toy cyclists you can move up and down on the maps of your own imagination. That liminal space had closed and there was only one outcome. With the harsh edges of the mountain starting to flux and blur in front of his eyes, Ferdy lost all motion.

Alex Burtin had squeezed himself out of the team car and was running – no, walking – alongside him, hurling encouragement, pushing Ferdy one final time. But Ferdy was in a trance. He was losing his battle against Ventoux, losing a battle against himself. He raged at spectators, swearing at them to get out of his way, swearing at Alex Burtin. Froth formed at the mouth as Louison Bobet rode past without a second look. Charly Gaul was next, then Ockers, then his teammates Huber and Clerici who didn't even bother to wait for him. Ferdy is finished. Ferdy not good.

And then he fell. He fell to the side of the path and remained there, ashen-faced, his legs still pedalling. Further down the mountain, Jean Mallejac, the Breton rider, was suffering the exact same fate, frothing at the mouth, grey-faced and hallucinating as the Tour Doctor tried to resuscitate him. Mallejac was taken away in an ambulance in between life and death, the Tour Doctor pressing on his chest, looking for signs of life, looking for the *soigneur* who had done this to him, who had given him the drugs – it can only be drugs.

That *soigneur*, coincidentally, was also Ferdy

Kübler's soigneur. Those bottles that would later be found in Mallejac's bedroom would also, coincidentally, be found in Ferdy Kübler's bedroom.

Ferdy lay at the side of the road, watching the wheels of lesser riders, riders who would never win a Tour nor even a stage or a Classic race. You can tell them by their bikes. They're just not as good. I need five minutes, he told himself. I need some water. I need to ride.

Wheels stopped passing by and Ferdy was momentarily left alone on the mountainside. Motorbikes slowed down to look at Ferdy and then accelerated away, kicking up dust as they went, dust that blew itself into Ferdy's motionless face. Voices came from stationary cars – where's Dr Dumas? He's gone into town with Mallejac. Looks like this one's had the same vitamins as Mallejac... someone give him some water at least. No, leave him be. The broom wagon's not far away now.

Come on Ferdy. Hop Ferdy, one last time. With a rush of blood, he pulled himself up, gave himself a couple of moments to gather himself, come to his senses. The mountain seemed to sway. Earthquake? He closed his eyes, squeezed them shut. The mountain remained still beneath his feet. He climbed back on his bike and rode the final few hundred metres to the summit and plummeted back into Avignon. Hard on the brakes, soft on the pedals, Ferdy rode with his temples throbbing, his head dizzy. The road bubbled up beneath him, stars encircled his vision. He found a bar, drank whatever they could give him, and got back on his bike, going the wrong way. They chased him down – Ferdy, Ferdy, where are you going? And they sent him back the right way.

He finished 42nd, a full 30 minutes behind the winner on the day, Louison Bobet. 30 minutes – is that all, he thought. It could have been two hours.

He lay in the bath that evening fulminating at the fate that had befallen him. Was his drink spiked? Had he mistakenly taken the same drugs that nearly killed poor Jean Mallejac? Had he got it all wrong? Ventoux is a mountain unlike any other, so he's heard. He can't say he hadn't been warned. He thought back to the wheel rims flashing past as he opened his eyes. They didn't seem to have any problems. Why could I not do it?

Ferdy is too old. Ferdy hurts too much.

Ferdy withdraws from the Tour, more out of shame than injury, beaten by Mont Ventoux, and reasons with himself that this is the last time he'll put his body through this. He reasons that as a responsible father, he must find other ways of earning his keep, that Mont Ventoux must mark the end of one road and the start of many others.

For many weeks, he considers Mont Ventoux his final humiliation, a capitulation. Until he speaks to Raphaël Géminiani on the telephone and agrees the legend of their conversation, the story they'll recount to journalists, the myth they'll sell of Ferdy's last stand on Mont Ventoux.

Who remembers what they really said to each other? What matters is the story.

TO CARACAS AND BACK

There comes a point of realisation, for cyclists of all disciplines, when they must consider a life beyond racing a bicycle. Study those who have gone before, and you will find many examples of men who have moved effortlessly from saddle to team directorships. Look for instance at Hans Martin, a man who surely must have been considering his post-racing career the minute he realised his actual racing career was heading for mediocrity. Look further back at the great Alfredo Binda, a man everyone here knows as Italian national team director, but in another lifetime, this was a rider so dominant they paid him *not* to ride the Giro d'Italia. Few in the modern peloton remember him as a rider, but all will have heard of his exploits.

Then there are those who disappear almost entirely from the sport. They run bars or restaurants, propping themselves up against the zinc while people hang on their every word, asking them about the framed photographs behind them – ah, this one, well if you insist... this was the day Fausto and I... and so on and so on.

And then there are men, in increasing numbers, who trade on their name in the business world. Ferdy has not yet dismantled his road bike; he will race in Italy and will profit from a few track appearances in 1956, but he has already signed contracts to represent companies across Europe, and one has even offered to use his famous nose as part of their advertising campaign. Well, if you've got it, flaunt it.

Ferdy and Rösli have been planning this for years. They must plan for the future, for the children. Ferdy must finish his autobiography, capitalise on the name Ferdy Kübler before some young upstart comes along and everyone forgets who you are. But no one will ever forget the name Ferdy Kübler if that famous nose is on every advertising hoarding along every road in Switzerland.

Sonja Koblet sees that famous nose, sees the book signings and the carefully planned post-racing life that the Küblers are enjoying and she fears for Hugo. Hugo has no plan for a life out of the saddle, unless that plan involves putting his name on a comb and trying to flog it at track meetings. The money comes in even though the results don't, but this is mostly through track meetings, and not the combs. You can still bank on the Koblet name, and occasionally he'll come up with a result or two.

And there's the problem. The word 'occasionally'. The wins are all too infrequent and the Koblets are reliant upon appearance money, negotiated up front with a 'who gives a damn about the money' attitude because Hugo is friends with everyone and friends don't talk money. Emil Keller knows that Hugo brings a certain audience along with him to his Hallenstadion venue, but they're not the young ones that come for Anquetil and Darrigade, the two bright things that everyone wants to see. But still, for Hugo, the money comes in.

It flows out, too. His mother's bakery is floundering, largely under the mismanagement of brother Adolf who comes begging for money every time he goes bankrupt. He can whip up a marvellous crème patissiere, but he doesn't know how to put a price on it. For now, Sonja turns a blind eye to Hugo's generosity, but she notes each outgoing for future reference. A bad month here, a broken oven at the bakery...

She knows that her looks will fade too, just as Hugo's hairline recedes. Her modelling contracts won't last forever, and that leaves her trading on what? Her husband's good name?

Look at Ferdy, she insists. Look at how he's coping. You have some years yet, but think about it.

Hugo thinks instead about Paris-Roubaix, about one more shot at glory on the mud-caked hell-roads of the north. There would be no mud in 1956, and there would be no glory either. He reached Wattignies with mechanical problems that were beyond his repair and beyond that of the team, and he watched Louison Bobet, saddle sores and all, sail off into the distance. The north of France is a solemn place to be when you're stood, alone in a field, listening to the wind whip around your ears and hoping that someone might appear with a spare wheel. Or a spare bike.

He would however lead a team of three in the Grand Prix de Ravenna, even at one point lapping that young whippersnapper Anquetil as he lay on the floor after a fall. You may have the looks, Jacques, but you don't have the prize. Could this be a sign of things to come? Was the old Hugo back? Or was this a new, more mature Hugo, ready to tackle the final years of his career with renewed strength and vigour?

There were signs at the Vuelta when in the third stage, Hugo slipped himself into the breakaway alongside both of the Bobets, Rik van Steenbergen, Federico Bahamontes and Miguel Poblet. He didn't win the sprint that day, but he was glad to have been part of the action, to have been in the leading group. Where he is meant to be. There would be more... in Albacete, he came fourth and the next day in Alicante, 2nd. 3rd in Valencia and then he won the 9th stage from Tarragona to Barcelona, seeing off van Steenbergen, Poblet, Padovan and Gilbert Bauvin with a tremendous sprint, overhauling van Steenbergen and Poblet at the very last. Ah, it had taken Spain to find the old Hugo!

Hugo loved the Vuelta. It was like the Tour but without the fanfare, without the fuss. Sure, there were crowds, but it had a down-at-heel feel, a dusty air about it. It was just the place for a revival. He could rub shoulders with his old peloton compadres, safe in the knowledge that he was their equal once more, and soon – should the ascendancy continue – he would be their better.

Alas, it was the next day as the heatwave returned to the Iberian peninsula, that he would lose four minutes on those compadres and that familiar feeling of his body shutting down, refusing to respond to his primitive urge to keep riding, came again. He withdrew halfway through the next stage from Tarrega to Zaragoza, climbing silently into the ambulance and refusing to tell anyone quite why he'd given up so soon. Because there was no single reason. How can you explain to everyone that you've stopped when you're not injured, you have no mechanical fault that prevents you from riding, you're just... not who you used to be. It is the culmination of so many small defects that have accumulated over the years, parts that haven't been repaired, red blood cells that will never return.

And here is the heartache of the roadman in decline. There's hope. Just enough hope to help you deny the inevitable, that you have been overtaken. One night you're beating the young boy everyone says reminds them of you – when you were young – and the next night you're exhausted, crying into your bidon. It's the hope that gets you.

You return to your villa and you hope that the next race will be the one. The one that feels easy, the one where you confirm that fleeting promise and you fulfil the pact you made with your adoring fans all those years ago, that you'd keep on riding, keep on giving them what they ask for. That you'd keep on giving your wife what she asks for, too.

Life also tends to get in the way the older a roadman gets. Whereas in previous years, Hugo would have spent half the year in hotels across Europe or South America, he was now spending more time at home. Sonja and his mother barely spoke and when they did it was with the glacial tone of the over-protective mother and the intrusive replacement of a wife. Summers that would have been spent getting away from all of this, riding around France with friends, were now summers spent wilfully ignoring Frau Koblet the elder's disdain for the *arriviste* Frau Koblet the younger, and trying to placate the latter.

Frau Koblet the elder had always adored her little Hugie. Less so her not-so-little Dolfi, the less successful brother who was running her boulangerie into the ground. More and more, Hugo found himself dragged into family conflicts when the only conflict he really desired was on two wheels. Why must I sit here listening to Adolf complaining about how I'm the favourite when I can be racing a bicycle and listening to nobody at all.

He returned to the track, to the adulation and the money, and that's where he stayed for the rest of the '56 season, wondering what it might take for his body to restore itself. Armin awaited him with open arms, and Hugo found himself in the unusual position of using summer to prepare for winter, a winter that saw them beat all comers at the Hallenstadion and the Vigorelli, including the unusual combination of Fausto Coppi and André Darrigade.

Still the money came in, if not with the flow of previous years, but it still flowed. The Koblets lived life to its fullest in the villa over Lake Zürich in between track meetings and their respective foreign duties, each of the Koblets eking out the last of their looks and limbs while people were still willing to pay for them. There was the thought of returning to the road, to the Giro d'Italia of 1957. It was only seven years ago that Hugo had won the Giro and he would be 32, an age at which a rider is supposed to be in his prime. He phoned around, suggesting to a few journalists that the Giro might be the ideal venue for Hugo Koblet to make his return to the big scene. He quickly regretted his words, especially on discovering that the Swiss would only be given a small team because, after all, their glory days are long behind them and the French are the foreigners everyone wants to see these days. The Italians were furious at first, even going so far as to send envoys to the Koblet villa for heated discussion, almost turning Hugo's head. They still want me. I still have a hand to play.

And then the Italians relented, allowing Hugo a larger Swiss contingent, before Hugo had more doubts, and just days before the Giro was due to start, he pulled out for good.

It was hard for people to be angry with Hugo. There was simply a bland disappointment, a shrug of 'well, he'll never be what he used to be' and on with the show. The words hurt more than the road itself.

There were some who suggested he enter the retirement home of tired cyclists, middle-distance track racing. There would be no hills, no mountains, no Grand Tours of 11 stages or longer, just revolutions behind a derny and the pay packets that would maintain the payments on the villa above Lake Zürich and the serial bankruptcies of brother Adolf and the Koblet boulangerie in Aussersihl.

Of all people, it was the taxman who took greatest interest in Hugo Koblet, turning up unannounced at the villa to enquire about where this and that painting had been enquired, asking how Hugo had performed at the *vel d'Hiv* one particular evening in 1953, what the bonuses might have been and has he, perhaps, filled in that form yet? Alas, no.

This was not Hugo's first run-in with the taxman. After his Tour de France win of 1951, a particularly charmless man had made himself at home in Hugo's bakery with a copy of Miroir des Sports and its estimation of Hugo's winnings in France, commenting on the earning potential of criteriums. They never miss a beat, thought Hugo. But back then, the money was flowing in from so many directions, he had men to handle these things for him, so he turned a blind eye.

This particular taxman had a drawer full of cyclists back at his office. He invited Hugo one day, although it wasn't really an invitation, more of a summons. "This one," he said, thrusting a picture of a vaguely recognisable former Swiss pro, "we ruined him. You all end up like this, paying back your winnings into the public purse. We'll make you pay your way, Hugo Koblet, one way or another."

There was no plan. There never had been a plan. Hugo left the tax office with his head spinning, like a drunk wandering the streets. The hope had all dried up and in its place was a constant questioning – what do I do now? Where do I go? Who do I become? And yet he carried on spending as if the money were still there, racking up debts and gambling with money that he'd borrowed, hoping that Sonja might not notice, that she'd carry on looking at the view over Lake Zürich and all would be fine in the end, as it always was.

Armin von Buren pleaded with Hugo to put some money aside, to stop the spending and stop bailing out his brother. Hugo just smiled and said "Armin, I won't live long. I just want to take advantage of what I've got."

He sold his Studebaker not long after, rejecting Armin's offer of 10,000 francs per month as a PR representative for his restaurant. Pride, perhaps, got in the way. A career with Armin in your service to be followed by what – a career in the service of Armin's restaurant?

Fortune didn't always flow in the opposite direction, though. An offer came to represent a consortium of Italian brands in Caracas, Venezuela. Caracas was boom-town and the Italians had always had a soft spot for Hugo. If he could represent Pirelli and Alfa

Romeo out there for a year or two, who knows what riches might await? And the Swiss taxman has no interest in what you make in Caracas, Hugo.

So he convinced Sonja that Caracas was the right move for them, perhaps they could start a family out there, enjoy the lifestyle while they're still young and the modelling contracts would flow for Sonja too. Caracas it is, Sonja demurred.

For two years, the Koblets lived, mostly happily, in Venezuela. Hugo would wear his best suit, enjoying the best American cars that Caracas had to offer, and would sell Alfa Romeos simply by being Hugo. The summers were long, the money adequate, and a life away from racing a bicycle wasn't perhaps as bad as Hugo had feared. It could sometimes be... happy. What he earned, he spent, and what he didn't spend he sent home to his mother and Adolf in the hope that it would keep the boulangerie afloat.

Sonja would have stayed, were it not for Hugo's mother falling ill and eventually succumbing to her illness in hospital. The Koblets rushed back from Caracas to witness Helene Koblet's final moments and to bury her. The Italian sponsors, always respectful of family, found Hugo work in Zürich, giving him two petrol stations to run, one of them conveniently outside the Oerlikon velodrome where Hugo had made his name. Why, a Hugo Koblet-run petrol station could be just the ticket for all of us, they said, and Hugo agreed.

At first, running a petrol station was easy. Old friends would appear as if from nowhere – would you fill her up, dear Hugo, it really is lovely to see you, oh look I appear to have forgotten my wallet – what's that? Next time? Oh Hugo you are a darling. Drop-for-drop, Hugo Koblet sold the cheapest petrol in all of Switzerland. His only trouble was being able to buy it in the first place, given that he gave so much of it away.

There were opportunities to return to the world of cycling, too. Commentary was one path, and he developed a good friendship with Sepp Renggli, but to all of those listening, this wasn't the Hugo they knew. There was no sparkle to his voice, and to those listening with the benefit of hindsight in later years, there was a note of regret. A tailing off at the end of sentences, a lack of confidence... like a light had gone out. There was even an incident where he poured a glass of water over Renggli for talking too much about Ferdy Kübler.

The taxman returned, and when he wasn't able to attend in person, he would send registered letters as his representatives. Still Hugo turned a blind eye, preferring instead to gamble, womanise and spend his way out of trouble. The bets might pay off, the women might soothe the pain. Sonja knew about the women – and to a degree, she endured it. But the question remained – why had the Koblets not started a family? Why had Sonja refused throughout the years in Caracas to give Frau Koblet a grandson, a mini Hugie.

Sonja, like so many of the women who preceded her, gradually began to see in Hugo a man who couldn't come to terms with his growing years. Like Frau Poehler, she saw a man who believed he was still a boy. Like Waltraut Haas, she saw a man who couldn't commit to anything beyond tomorrow. The money had gone, the women around Hugo were getting younger, and for Sonja, the marriage was as good as over. You can only wait so long for a man to mature. Hugo would never grow up.

Hugo moved into the studio flat above the petrol station, sleeping in his overalls and smelling of oil as the postman knocked on the door, shouting through the letterbox that he can see the Alfa Romeo parked outside, he knows Herr Koblet is at home, that there are letters sent by registered post that absolutely must be signed today. Did he know that one of those registered letters held within its envelope the divorce papers issued by the soon-to-be-ex-Frau Koblet? Or did he know that they were mostly courtesy of the taxman, now taking an even more forensic interest in the revenues of Hugo's failing petrol stations and criteriums raced many years previously?

Hugo had driven up to the old villa on Monday, where Sonja was still living and he had pleaded with her to take him back. He remembered how he had dropped to his knees, how he had promised to change without every really knowing how to change, or if change were even possible. Time was he'd make a promise and it would just happen. No more.

Hugo hauled himself out of bed, picked up the keys to the Alfa, got in the car and sped off, leaving the postman and his registered letters behind.

Town turned to countryside which turned to forest as Hugo propelled the Alfa down empty lanes, through empty towns, destination nowhere in particular.

Had suicide been on his mind? Or was it the culmination of this series of conclusive failures? All Hugo knew was that there was nothing left to live for, nothing left to fight for. The spirit had long since drained from his body, taking with it the hope of revival. But ending it all – had the thought really passed through Hugo's mind? They were perhaps throwaway thoughts at first, never anything serious. But then – if there really is nothing better to come, if the only life to be led is that of a debtor, then why carry on at all?

And is it ever a decision? Is it just a series of events that culminate in a choice that, once apparent, is a toss of a coin. Hugo felt both isolated and surrounded, threatened on all sides while those who once supported and adored him had moved on, found younger subjects on which to foist their affections. Or they found him irrelevant. He had found meaning in a sport that idolised fortitude and courage, that had made legends out of men of granite. And yet when those men of granite are left at the side of the road, they erode over time. They chip slowly at the edges.

The first signs of erosion dated back to 1952. That injection, Hugo told everyone, it put ten years on me. Hugo fought endlessly to find the Hugo who rode before the injection. He threw himself down mountains in search of that man only now to discover that this pre-injection Hugo no longer exists. So why should the post-injection Hugo exist? This new Hugo, the one who lacks character and fortune, why should he exist?

Decisions like this are made easier when you become the third person.

Hugo accelerated further, down long expanses of leaf-strewn country road. Perhaps, at the end of this stretch, something will appear. Something that gives me hope. Instead, the drab, post-brown mush of late autumn offers nothing but decay. Low sunlight is muzzled by grey blankets of cloud. The Alfa drives on and Hugo winds the window down, feels the chill of November air whipping against his cheeks.

The end will come anyway. It always does. The question is whether it comes for you, or you come for it. You don't make these decisions and hold yourself to it, you don't pass the minutes considering with certainty your imminent departure from the earthly. You hover, you hesitate, you consider that for the final time, you are considering something, that this is to be human and that if perhaps you were to make a different choice, things might turn out differently.

But then you remember that this is hope, and hope is for other people.

You don't enter this pact with yourself blindly. You reason with yourself. What do I lose, what do other people lose? What do I gain? If I do it, will it be quick? If not quick, will it be certain? There are some who would accuse him of a cry for help if it's not conclusive, but then to whom would Hugo cry now?

There is a tree, standing apart from the others, near a sawmill. Hugo sees it and drives past, considers it for a moment and brakes, hard. He does a u-turn and drives past again at speed. Does he think, at that moment, that driving into a tree is the way out? That this would be decisive action? He drives past again, does another u-turn and accelerates past once more.

Don't be a fool, Hugo. This is the coward's way out.

The pulse is racing. What choice do I have? Who would miss me? I have bowed out of so many lives, so many people have moved on from Hugo Koblet. Even I have moved on from Hugo Koblet.

He closes his eyes, grasps the wheel, and without braking, without fear, he leaves the road.

GOODBYE HUGO KOBLET

FERDY: The nurses told me that it might be useful, Hugo, my talking. That you might not respond but that you'd hear me. I hope you have heard some of it, and I hope that you managed not to hear all of it. I can talk quite a lot, you know this. Ferdy likes to talk.

They also say that you might not come out of your coma, that your injuries are too serious. This might be news to you, I'm sorry. I guess someone has to tell you.

Armin told me that you were half a million in debt, that you were gambling and that Adolf kept asking for money and you kept giving it, even when you didn't have it to give. We didn't look after you, Hugo. We didn't do enough. We didn't see the signs and we didn't rally round like we could have done.

We have all let you down. We should have been there more often, even just to go for a ride. Do you remember what it's like just to ride your bicycle, not to push it too hard?

I threw myself into not-cycling so hard because it was all I could do to forget racing, to forget how full that life was when the road felt it would never end. It was so hard, Hugo, to go from one day being famous for what you do best, to being a complete novice at everything you do. Whoever prepares us for what comes afterwards?

You know what I missed most of all? Not having to think. The absence of conscious thought. Ah, I bet you're thinking Ferdy's off on another of his famous philosophies! But I miss that, still today. All these years after hanging up my racing bike, I miss the not-thinking. Sometimes I do go out, back up into the mountains, just to block out the constant thinking, the people talking to me, the constant 'what comes next'.

I just never thought you'd be struggling with that too. I just thought – oh Hugo, he'll be fine. He'll be fine. Beautiful Hugo they called you, they thought you'd go on forever.

Look at me. I'm talking here as if you committed suicide. Perhaps you didn't. Perhaps it was a deer, there are deer in that forest, you may have been startled by one, you may have tried to avoid it. Or you hit a patch of oil in the road. These things are known to happen.

But you didn't brake.

I've been to that tree. I've stood underneath it, wondering what possessed you to do this, whether you did this actively at all. If you had braked, there would be tyre marks.

Hugo, you took that car and you drove it straight into a tree without braking. I sense this is what you wanted.

It will be my lifelong regret I couldn't help you choose another option. Perhaps we'll ride again, Hugo. I'll look for you when it's my time.

Hugo's Alfa Romeo hit the pear tree at 120km per hour, destroying the car instantly and leaving Hugo in between life and death. On hearing the terrible noise, one man, the first to the scene, hurried out to the grass verge and saw Hugo's bloodied limbs protruding from the crumpled door. Hugo was still conscious; he tried to speak to him.

"Let me die," Hugo murmured, before falling unconscious.

Emile Isler cleared the broken branches from the car and pulled Hugo from the wreckage. He had memories of learning first aid when he was in the military; he put Hugo in a recovery position. Cars passed without stopping as Emile Isler ran back inside to call the emergency services and he stood watching, arms folded behind his back as the ambulance came, followed by a series of police cars and eventually, curious onlookers. Nobody spoke to Emile Isler, nobody asked him how he came to be covered in Hugo's blood, or how Hugo came to be lying on the grass verge, or even how Hugo's car came to be wrapped around the pear tree in the first place. Emile Isler simply changed his clothes, went back to work, and carried on with his day. When someone told him that the model Sonja Koblet was looking to speak to him and possibly whether he could come out and speak to her, he replied that Sonja Koblet could come to him and speak, but she never did.

For days, the idea of suicide was barely mentioned. The very idea. It was a road accident, they said. You get a lot of deer round here. And yet Hugo, who had never been involved in anything worse than some scraped bodywork in a race with Louison Bobet, who was known to everyone as a more-than-capable driver, had somehow misjudged a simple curve in the road, had somehow forgotten to apply the brakes and had gone headlong into a pear tree. Oh, it could only have been an accident. And to have crossed the ditch in between road and verge, how could he have achieved this small feat? His odds of hitting that tree were what – a hundred to one? Suicide, indeed. What a strange way to go.

And yet, did anyone actually know Hugo anymore? The Hugo they knew loved life too much to commit suicide. The Hugo they knew was still laughing with Louison and bargaining with Bartali, a smile on his face. The Hugo they knew was chasing women at criteriums, spending money in casinos, buying himself new cars. That's Hugo. Why would Hugo not want to carry on this playboy lifestyle?

The surgeons did all they could. Hugo had suffered a broken skull, multiple fractures in his legs and his foot had been ripped out by the force of the impact. They operated for several hours and operated in hope. Dr Kübler, irony upon ironies, confided to surrounding reporters that Hugo is alive and while he may be in a critical condition, he could survive this. Tuesday offered some hope, but Wednesday offered little in response. Hugo's condition worsened and he returned to his coma. Another surgeon carried out an operation on Hugo's skull while Hugo's own Dr Rupf looked on, tears in his eyes, weighing up Hugo's chances at an optimistic 2%.

Hugo slipped further into the coma on the Thursday while visitors sat by his side, some for hours, saying nothing, others talking in the hope that Hugo might hear them, that Hugo might give some sign of life if they were to stimulate memories of years gone by.

Early on Friday morning, Hugo's heart stopped beating, his pain ended. His funeral took place four days later at the same church in which he and Sonja had married ten years earlier. The same faces were there – Ferdy Kübler, who else. Louison Bobet, Jean Robic, flowers from Gino Bartali and Jacques Anquetil in their absence. Thousands had gathered outside to wish Hugo goodbye, lining the streets in silent sorrow. Disbelief. Hundreds more had laid flowers at the foot of the pear tree.

A little later, Sonja attended Hugo's cremation with his family and returned, alone, to the villa overlooking Lake Zürich.

THE
PEAR
TREE

Emile Isler watched winter come and go, and did that pear tree outside his sawmill bear flowers? Not one, not the next spring nor the next, nor indeed any spring after that.

The tree stood by the roadside, a pear tree in all but name.

And did anyone come to the tree after Hugo's death? Sure, once the flowers had been removed, a few girls stood crying underneath the tree, but the harsh winter that followed was enough to put a halt to their vigil. Emile sometimes thought about going to comfort them, but he wouldn't have known what to say. He wasn't that kind of man.

There was one man, though. Emile saw him through the fence. He was dressed in a long black overcoat, formal trousers underneath. Good shoes. The man had his hair parted to the side; he had a large nose. He stood underneath the tree for a good hour, his head bowed. At times, he seemed to be talking to the tree. Mostly, he was silent. The wind blew the branches around his head.

Emile called out to his wife. Come look, this man has been there for half an hour already. Do you think he's someone important?

Before the man left, he took a knife from his pocket and cut some bark from the tree. Little shavings of bark from a pear tree that no longer bears pears, into which a man drove his car. This world, Emile Isler thought to himself, why do I not understand it? He left the smart man with his large nose and his side-parting to his strange business with the tree and returned to his work.

Pieces of that pear tree found their way into the palms of old acquaintances of Hugo Koblet. Waltraut Haas, for one, has a slither of bark on her mantelpiece, given to her by Ferdy Kübler one evening. He had arrived on her doorstep, soaked and sodden by the December rain, his coat dripping on the doormat. He asked that she take it, that she help him ensure that nobody forgets the name Hugo Koblet. That his memory is retained. She said nothing, she just took the offering and nodded, which is what Ferdy did, before turning his back on her and departing.

Mariandl watched from her window as the broad-shouldered outline of Ferdy Kübler trudged disconsolately back to his car, and she watched as he sat at the wheel for what must have been five minutes, maybe ten, wondering what to do, where to go, who to see next.

And with a deep breath, Ferdy Kübler pulled out and drove cautiously down the road. Mariandl watched as the lights of his car faded into the distance and Ferdy Kübler, too, was gone from her life.

AFTERWORD

That Hugo Koblet committed suicide shouldn't really be in any doubt. There are suggestions of a suicide note, although none has been made public, and his last words - to Emile Isler - were "let me die."

That Hugo Koblet felt he had to commit suicide, however, is another question altogether. Or, indeed, that he had contemplated it when he got in his car that November morning. We can only surmise what was going through his mind that day, and that is what I have attempted to do here.

What is certain is that Hugo was suffering from mental health problems that today would have been more quickly identified and, you would hope, resolved. You would hope that networks of friends and acquaintances would pick up on the signs, would offer themselves as support. We are more finely attuned to mental health issues today.

Or are we? I look at the cases of Naomi Osaka and Simone Biles, even at cricketers such as Marcus

Trescothick and Ben Stokes, and I see plenty of evidence that we have some way to go. Would Hugo Koblet have survived in the modern world with its social media networks spitting venom at sports stars who fail to live up to the expectations of fans, or even the expectations they put upon themselves?

Hugo's career mirrors that of so many riders, footballers, tennis players and cricketers. A fleeting peak, cruelly snatched away from him and a long, unfortunate coda during which he struggles vainly to recapture the essence of his youthful peak. What is doubly cruel is that Hugo's peak was stolen from him by Carl Senn and his 'Dirty Doctor' with their vials of Akzedron. He has to learn how to manage his decline, only to find his great rival Ferdy Kubler is already managing his with enormous success.

Ferdy is often depicted as Hugo's 'diametrical opposite'. Where Hugo is depicted as a dove, Ferdy is an eagle. Where Hugo is gifted, Ferdy is a grafter. Hugo is jazz where Ferdy is an Alpine horn. And so on, and so on. Their rivalry is what finally drove Ferdy to rein in his instincts and manage his resources better. At first, Hugo appears to be mildly amused by his elder, but as Hugo's decline sets in, the pendulum swings and Ferdy is an annoyance. The contrasts are emphasised once more - Hugo is a gentleman, Ferdy doesn't pay his bills... Hugo drives fast cars, Ferdy doesn't have a car.

And eventually, despite everything, the two men became friends. It is Ferdy who is there in the background on Hugo's last night at the Hallenstadion velodrome, all smiles and brylcream. It is Ferdy who takes Hugo to London for Six Day races as their careers become more of a tribute act to the Golden Era of racing. Waltraut Haas tells of the day "Hugo's great friend Ferdy Kubler came round and gave me a piece of bark from the pear tree, asking me to keep this so that his memory is retained forever."

But while Ferdy managed his post-racing career successfully, eventually spending his days negotiating business contracts and teaching people how to ski, Hugo couldn't find his position in the world. He went to Venezuela, because he was asked to. He took control of two petrol stations, because they were offered to him. He continued to womanise, to gamble and to search in vain for the life he used to have while younger men like Jacques Anquetil won multiple Tours de France with the simplicity that he had found in 1951.

We can't all have the inner strength and forward planning of a Ferdy Kubler. Life comes at you like it came at Hugo Koblet, and you can't always be ready for it. You can't always adapt. You need help. It is available, if you need it.

If you're in the UK and you wish to talk to the Samaritans, you can do so on 116 123. In the US, the National Suicide Hotline can be reached on 988.

I hope this book has, at the very least, revived the legends of Ferdy Kubler and Hugo Koblet, two of the greatest cyclists the world has ever known.

Hugo Koblet, 12th July 1954,
Nederlands: Collectie / Archief : Fotocollectie Anefo

Ferdy with Roger Hassenforder ahead of the start of the 1954
Tour de France
Foto Ben van Meerendonk / AHF, collectie IISG, Amsterdam

Hugo Koblet, 1951
Fotocollectie Anefo. Nationaal Archief, Den Haag, nummertoegang 2.24.01.03, bestanddeelnummer 904-6496.

Hugo & Ferdy, 1952

Ferdy and Hugo line up together for the 'Battle of the Two K's'
in the 1954 Tour de France

Fotocollectie Anefo. Nationaal Archief, Den Haag,
nummertoegang 2.24.01.03, bestanddeelnummer 906-5928.

Top-left: Ferdy wins the first stage of the 1947 Tour de France in Lille (Nederlands: Collectie / Archief : Fotocollectie Anefo)

Bottom-left: Ferdy outpaces Breton rider Mahe on the same stage, 1947 (Nederlands: Collectie / Archief : Fotocollectie Anefo)

Top right: Hugo and Ferdy promoting local brands at the Hallenstadion Velodrome, 1957 (ETH-Bibliothek Zürich, Bildarchiv / Fotograf: Comet Photo AG (Zürich) / Com_C06-125-006 / CC BY-SA 4.0)

Lightning Source UK Ltd.
Milton Keynes UK
UKHW010755080422
401285UK00003B/390